The Philippine Cookbook

The Philippine Cookbook

Reynaldo Alejandro

A Perigee Book

A Perigee Book
A division of Penguin Group (USA) Inc.
375 Hudson Street
New York, New York 10014

First edition: June 1985

Library of Congress Cataloging-in-Publication Data

Alejandro, Reynaldo G.
    The Philippine cookbook.
    Includes index.
    1. Cookery, Philippine.   I. Title.
[TX724.5.P5A43   1985]   641.59599   84-18926
ISBN 978-0-399-51144-8

Cover photograph copyright © 1982 by William Pell Studio
Food Stylist: Betty Pell

This book conceived and produced in conjunction with
The Photographic Book Company, Inc.

PRINTED IN THE UNITED STATES OF AMERICA
40   39   38

Dedication

To my grandmother, for all the time spent
teaching me in her kitchen, and to Lee for his spiritual
nourishment and patience.

Acknowledgments

Without the help, encouragement and guidance of the following people, this book could not have been written. Sincerest thanks to: Nonon Padilla, Cora Yabut Custodio, Marisita Yuson, Rose Vallejo, May Mayor and Louie Acosta, who helped in the preliminary research. Presy Pascual and Virginia Alejandro for the oral history tapes of my grandmother. Tessie Centenera, Eli Lovina, Eddie Cruz, Maria Clara Magparangalan, Andy Paras, Leticia Shehani, Rita Gerona-Adkins and Cora Sibal for sharing their recipes. The staff of The Photographic Book Company, especially Linda Weinraub, Kevin Clark and Larry Marquez for the actual production of the book. Jennie Zamora and Liwayway O'Boyle, my esteemed friends, whose kitchens witnessed the stages of the various recipes tested. Chris Hawver, Charlie Santangelo, May Mayor and Carl Parisi, my fellow chefs. Robert Posch, Nick Malgieri and Michael Bradshaw, my culinary teachers, for their insights and valuable advice. Glenda Barretto, Millie Reyes, Gilda Cordero-Fernando, Ado Escudero, Doreen and Willi Fernandez— my beloved Filipino colleagues. Ministry of Tourism (N.Y.). And most especially to Herb Taylor and Cora Sibal, whose foresight and dedication made this book possible.

Contents

About the Illustrations

The illustrations in this book are derived from the Filipino folk art of papercutting. The origins of this delicate craft are obscure, but fragile cutout designs of flowers, vines, fruits and vegetables have graced festive Filipino tables since the early nineteenth century. Complicated scenes depicting animals, birds, rice paddies and dwellings, as well as seasonal greetings spelled out in paper, are also part of the craft of papercutting.

Traditionally, the cutout designs were created as part of the wrappings for fine homemade candies called *pastillas. Papel de Japon*, a delicate, tissue-like, multicolored paper is used and tiny, razor-sharp scissors snip out the delicate patterns. Patience is the key to mastering the craft of papercutting, which is most often practiced by older women, who seem to have more of the required virtue. In the Bulacan region north of Manila these women have turned their skill and patience into a cottage industry that supplies most of the Philippines with the cutout designs.

The cutouts used to produce the illustrations in this book were created by Mrs. Luisa Abelardo Arguelles.

Introduction

Imagine a rich, dark, well-marinated stew of chicken and pork, with flavors that hint of the vinegar and soy sauce in the marinade.

Imagine a steaming mound of sautéed noodles with bits of fresh vegetables, thinly sliced savory sausage and tiny shrimp laced throughout.

Imagine a whole chicken boned and stuffed with a mixture of ground chicken, pork and ham plus whole sausages and hard-boiled eggs, so that when it is sliced and served, the dish looks as good as it tastes.

This is Philippine cooking at its finest! These mouth-watering dishes are just a sample of some of the delights that await the culinary explorer. But much of the exploration will be on familiar territory, because Spanish and Chinese influences are everywhere. And the exploration will not be an arduous trek, because Filipino cooking is easy.

Philippine cuisine is the familiar blended with the exotic, and to understand it better requires some knowledge of the country's history and its cultural influences. Just as Filipino people are part Malay, Chinese and Spanish, so is the cuisine of their seven-thousand-island nation.

History

The Malays were among the first inhabitants of the archipelago over twenty thousand years ago. Land bridges that are now under the sea made the migration possible.

Chinese traders may have sailed their junks across the Yellow Sea as early as 300 A.D. Certainly by the year 1000, trading was taking place on a regular basis with the coastal colonies the Chinese were establishing. By 1400, they had moved inland and were finally established as part of the culture.

In 1521, Ferdinand Magellan discovered the Philippines for the Western world, and a period of Spanish influence began that lasted over three hundred years. Those years had a lasting and monumental effect on the Philippines.

With the departure of the Spanish in 1898, the Philippines came under the influence of the United States. Americans brought a new language, new influences and some new ideas to the cuisine of the islands, which by then had become as rich and varied as the culture.

American Influences

In the period following World War II, surplus canned foods became widely available to Filipinos because of the shortages of fresh produce and the black market. The Filipinos embraced these "new foods" and turned them into dishes that taste nothing like canned food. By sautéing canned corned beef with onions and garlic, they created a dish uniquely their own. Before the Japanese invasion, American food influences came in the form of institutional-style salads and pies. Construction companies, mining companies and military installations employed Filipinos, who brought home the wonders of potato and macaroni salads and fruit pies. Although the Filipino versions of these salads have lots of chicken and some vegetables not found in the United States, they are nevertheless as "American as apple pie" in shape, size and texture.

Spanish Influences

Spanish additions to the cuisine are hard *not* to find. It has been said that the origin of about 80 percent of the dishes prepared in the Philippines today can be traced to Spain. In fact, many Filipino dishes have Spanish names; oddly enough, some of them aren't even Spanish! Most important, though, the Spaniards introduced tomatoes and garlic as well as the gentle art of sautéing them with onions in olive oil. Whether or not Mexican cooking influenced Philippine cuisine is a subject for debate (see box).

The Mexican Connection

The Philippines came under Spanish control due to two factors: the discovery of the islands by Magellan and the division of the world into two hemispheres by Pope Alexander VI to appease Spain and Portugal (the two feuding Catholic world powers). In the sixteenth century, all that lay east of the line drawn down the middle of the Atlantic Ocean was given to Portugal and all that lay west of the line was given to Spain. The dividing line placed the Philippines, exactly halfway around the globe, under Spanish control. Since Spain had to sail west to get to its Pacific possessions, the Philippine islands were administered through Mexico for more than two hundred years. Galleons regularly plied the waters between Acapulco and Manila, bringing necessities and modified Spanish influences.

Today in Mexico there is a paste of vinegar, oil, chili, spices and herbs. It is used in pork dishes such as puerco en adobo and chuletas de puerco adobadas. Today in the Philippines, *adobo* is the closest thing the country has to a national dish. It consists of chicken and pork that has been marinated and stewed in a mixture of vinegar, soy sauce, garlic and peppercorns. Is this just a coincidence, or did the Mexicans also contribute to the cuisine of the Philippines?

Chinese Influences

Chinese contributions are all-pervasive, too, with noodle dishes heading the list. Generically, noodle dishes are known as *pansit*. Pansit, however, can come in many forms, and the variations have little in common other than that some kind of noodle is used. Dumplings — *siomai* — and egg rolls — *lumpia* — are the more popular forms of food that have come from China. Also very Chinese is the wide array of dipping sauces that often accompany Filipino dishes. Served in tiny saucerlike plates, these sauces enhance the foods they're served with to precise, individually determined degrees.

Malay Influences

The Malay effects on the cuisine are harder to trace but can be found in many of the so-called indigenous recipes—especially those in which coconut and coconut milk are important ingredients. Some of the more exotic regional specialties may be Malay-influenced: like Kare-Kare (oxtails in peanut sauce), Pinakbet (wild greens, bits of pork and fermented fish in coconut milk) and Dinuguan (a dark stew made with pork blood and flavored with whole hot peppers).

Whole roast pig, now known by its Spanish name *lechón*, may have found its way to the table via the sacrificial altar of these ancient people who inhabited the islands. Chickens, too, were offered in early Malay ritual, and this may have led to the many chicken dishes of today.

Rice and Fish

The mainstay of the Philippine diet is simply rice and fish. Indeed, most Filipinos survive on little else. Rice has been grown in the Philippines for over two thousand years, and the original inhabitants probably fished the surrounding seas for a long time before that.

Over twenty varieties of rice are grown in the Philippines today, and the language has hundreds of words to describe rice and its characteristics.

There are many varieties of rice other than the familiar long- and short-grain classifications. Some are cultivated for their fragrance or whiteness, others for their glutinous quality. One variety yields bluish-purple grains; another has a strong nutty flavor. Filipinos, however, have a preference for white and fragrant rice, and in former times, a gift of a sack of "bigas de San Nicolas" from San Nicolas in Ilocos Norte, was highly appreciated because it had both these desirable qualities and it was scarce.

The importance of rice can be discerned from the role it plays in myths, legends and religious rituals. In the Philippines, the Zambal, Tingguian and Tiruray tribes have many folk tales concerning rice. The descendants of the creators of the Banaue rice terraces (see box) continue to believe that rice has a soul. In the lowlands, the cultivation of rice continues to govern the daily life of the peasants, and the pre-Hispanic rituals and reverence for rice were carried over into Philippine observance of Christian holidays and feasts of saints.

Fish, too, has always been a basic food. Over two thousand species of fish are found in the waters surrounding the islands, and the variety of crabs, lobsters and shrimps is astounding.

In addition to the bountiful resource of the ocean, the Filipinos have another source of protein—freshwater fish ponds. Though aquaculture, the raising of fish and shellfish under controlled conditions, may be new in some areas of the world, that activity has been going on in the Philippines for at least a thousand years. Fish ponds supply the population with over twenty varieties of fish, crabs, shrimps, oysters and other shellfish. The milkfish, *bangus*, is one of the most popular fish raised in ponds in the Philippines, and with good reason. Its flesh is white, solid and delicious, and it lends itself to many satisfying meals.

Rice Terraces

Four thousand feet up the steep-sided mountains of northern Luzon's Central Cordillera mountains cling the world-famous rice terraces of Banaue. Often called the eighth wonder of the world, the terraces are an engineering marvel that cover 100 square miles.

They were started about 1000 B.C. by people who came from southern China and northern Vietnam, where similar terraces are found. They were first used for the cultivation of taro and millet and then later for rice.

Today the local tribe, the Ifugao, maintain the innumerable small paddies with rock retaining walls and keep them irrigated with the water that flows from the top of the terraces into the valley. In January, they plant the rice; by March, all the terraces are green. As the rice matures, it takes on a golden color, and the terraces are transformed. Harvest and the ritual thanksgiving ceremonies follow in June and July. August, September and October see the paddies repaired and prepared for the sowing of the seeds in November and December.

The Ifugaos believe that rice has a soul. Seeing the terraces makes it easy to believe this.

Archeological evidence has shown that the first Filipinos ate small deer, pig, several different small mammals and shellfish. Today Filipinos eat hamburgers, pizza and french fries along with their traditional foods. The cuisine is a lively and ever-changing aspect of the Filipino culture. It has been evolving for over thirty thousand years, and its heritage is rich.

Note: The Philippine archipelago comprises some 7,000 islands, each one having a distinct language or dialect. For obvious reasons, a *lingua franca* is used. This is Tagalog, the dialect of Luzon, the main island where the capital, Manila, is located. Tagalog is spoken throughout the Philippines, along with the local dialect and English, which is the language of instruction in all government-run schools. Many Spanish terms are also used, although not exactly as the Spanish would, and occasionally transliterated to accommodate the Tagalog rules of spelling.

1

The Basics of Philippine Cooking

Philippine cooking is surprisingly simple; no special utensils are needed. Even a wok, which is commonly used in the Philippines and is almost essential for Chinese cooking, can be done without for most Philippine dishes.

No special skills are needed, either. If you can prepare American dishes, you can prepare the food of the Philippines. In fact, most of the dishes that follow are either sautéed or stewed. Other dishes are boiled, braised or fried. Baked dishes are rare, which is perfectly sensible for a tropical cuisine.

Some common terms and methods of cooking follow; the Glossary contains a more complete listing.

adobo — cooked in vinegar, soy sauce and garlic

guisado — sautéed

sinigang — boiled with a sour fruit or vegetable

paksiw — cooked in vinegar and garlic

estofado — prepared with a burnt-sugar sauce.

ginataan — cooked in coconut milk

rellenado — stuffed

sarciado — with a sauce

Two styles of preparing food in the Philippines are part of the cuisine not only because of their delicious taste but also because they keep well without refrigeration. Dishes cooked *adobo* or *sinigang* style are preserved because of the effect of the vinegar or souring ingredient. In rural tropical areas, this makes storing leftovers possible. Dishes prepared in both these manners seem to improve when stored, so it is a good idea to prepare large amounts to ensure having leftovers.

In many of the recipes that follow, vegetable ingredients that are used may be difficult to locate in ordinary food stores or supermarkets. But most major metropolitan centers have "chinatowns" or Oriental neighborhoods where all the ingredients can be purchased. In smaller cities, "Oriental stores" can often be located by checking the local Yellow Pages under Oriental or Filipino stores.

One of the ingredients that may prove difficult to locate is *patis*. Patis is a very salty, thin, amber-color fish or shrimp sauce that is sold in bottles under various brand names. *Nuoc mam* is the Vietnamese equivalent, and *nampla* is the Thai equivalent.

Though patis is commonly used in many dishes in the Philippines, it is marked as an optional ingredient in all the recipes in this book because the flavor it imparts takes some getting used to. Its pungent odor and strong flavor put it into the category of "acquired tastes." Salt is its closest and best substitute.

Among the other ingredients commonly used in main dishes that are not readily available in local food markets but that may be found in Oriental or Hispanic food stores are the following:

Coconut milk and coconut cream can be bought in 6- or 12-ounce cans.

Anatto seeds, commonly known in the Philippines as *achuette* or *achiote,* may be bought in 4- or 8-ounce bottles.

Banana blossoms or flowers are clusters of matchlike flowers found inside a banana pod. Dried banana blossoms are sold in most Oriental food stores.

Bagoong, or shrimp paste made from small salted and fermented shrimps, is sold in jars in Oriental food stores.

Chorizo de Bilbao, a Spanish sausage used in most Spanish-influenced meat stews, is sold in most Hispanic stores; however, a good substitute is pepperoni or any other spicy sausage like the Polish kielbasa.

Dried Chinese mushrooms and Chinese sausages can be bought in most Oriental food stores. Salted black beans can be bought in cans or packages, also in Oriental food stores.

Other Oriental ingredients such as bean curd, Chinese cabbage, a Chinese vegetable called *bak choy* and even some Chinese egg and bean noodles are now available in local food markets in big cities on the East and West coasts of the United States.

Even though some of the more exotic vegetables called for in some dishes simply are not available in the United States, adequate substitutes are everywhere. For the most part, all the ingredients and spices can be found in a well-stocked food market.

The Filipino Taste

Organizing a cookbook of Filipino cuisine along traditional lines forces dishes into categories that do not really exist in the native culture.

When a Filipino sits down to eat a meal, it is all there—all at once—appetizers, soup, main dishes, desserts—to be eaten randomly, at will. Some Filipinos when traveling abroad become frustrated with the traditional (Western) method of serving food a course at a time.

A particular hardship is to have to wait until the end of the meal for something sweet, since dishes that many Westerners would call desserts would be considered a main part of the meal by Filipinos. In fact, a popular Filipino breakfast dish is a chocolate-flavored porridge of glutinous rice served with dried smoked fish and sweetened rice cakes topped with coconut flakes.

The Filipino taste is accustomed to contrasts and distinct flavors. Bitter, sour, salty, fishy and meaty flavors are very much part of the cuisine. Filipinos also appreciate the subtle flavors that are produced when a number of foods are slowly sauteed or gently stewed together. The Filipino taste understands the use of garlic, ginger and onion; and the subtle differences of rock salt versus fine salt and black pepper versus white pepper; and the merits of laurel and oregano; and the importance of saffron, sugar, soy sauce, fish sauce and all the other flavors acquired from the various cultures that have touched it.

2
Appetizers

The recipes in this section would normally be served as side dishes to accompany main dishes of pork, beef, vegetables, poultry or fish. However, salted shrimp fries, pork and chicken skin cracklings and fried squid strips all make excellent beginnings for any Filipino meal.

Some dishes that are traditionally main dishes in the Philippines have been adapted to serve as appetizers. Crabs-in-their-Shells, Lumpia Shanghai (egg rolls), Lumpiang Ubod (fresh egg rolls) and Siomai (boiled dumplings) are all in this category.

Lumpia Shanghai
• Philippine Fried Egg Rolls, Shanghai Style

½ pound ground pork
½ pound shrimps, chopped fine
½ cup chopped water chestnuts
½ cup green onions, chopped
   fine
1 teaspoon salt
1 teaspoon freshly ground
   pepper
1 egg
1 tablespoon soy sauce
1 package egg roll wrappers (sold
   in Oriental stores)
½ cup cooking oil

Combine pork, shrimp, water chestnuts, green onion, egg and soy sauce. Season with salt and pepper. Place a level tablespoon of filling on each egg roll wrapper and seal with a few drops of water. Deep-fry in hot oil and drain on paper towel. Serve with sweet-and-sour sauce (see page 202).

Fresh Lumpia • Fresh Egg Roll

½ pound shrimps
¼ pound pork, boiled for 15 minutes
1 can of bamboo shoots or hearts
   of palm (optional)
salt and pepper
10 lettuce leaves
2 cloves garlic, crushed
1 medium-size onion, diced
1 teaspoon salt
1 teaspoon freshly ground
   pepper
fresh lumpia wrapper (see
   directions)

Devein shrimps and cut into small pieces. Cut pork into small pieces. Cut bamboo shoots or hearts of palm into thin long strips.

Sauté garlic, diced onion, shrimp and pork, for about 10 minutes. Then add bamboo shoots or hearts of palm, salt and pepper to taste, and cook for another 5 minutes. Drain well.

On a plate, lay wrapper flat, place a segment of lettuce leaf on wrapper, then put about 2 tablespoons of filling on top of lettuce leaf and roll wrapper. Seal with a little water and place edges down. Serve with lumpia sauce and crushed garlic.

Lumpia Sauce

4 tablespoons cornstarch
⅓ cup brown sugar
¼ cup soy sauce
1½ cups water
crushed garlic

Combine cornstarch, sugar, soy sauce and water. Cook 5 minutes over low heat, stirring constantly to prevent lumps. When done, serve with crushed garlic.

Fresh Lumpia Wrapper

    1   cup flour
    1   egg
    1   cup water

2 duck eggs   1 c water   1/2 C cornstarch dispersed in 1 c. water

Mix all ingredients until very smooth.

    Lightly grease a non-stick pan and heat. Brush mixture onto pan. When dough starts to come away from the pan, lift wrapper out carefully. It will not lift out if mixture is not done.

Yield: 10 pieces.

Fried Calamares • Fried Squid Strips

2 pounds fresh or frozen squid,
  cleaned and cut into round
  strips
1 teaspoon salt
1 cup all-purpose flour
½ cup cooking oil

Drain squid strips very well. Pat dry with paper towels. Season with salt. Put flour in a small paper bag and shake squid strips in it, a few at a time. In a medium skillet, heat oil and fry squid strips, dropping them in one at a time. Fry until golden brown and crisp. Drain on paper towel.

Serves 4–6.

Chicharon • Pork Cracklings

2 pounds pork rind, cut into
  1-inch squares
3 cups water
1 tablespoon salt
1 cup vegetable or corn oil

Boil cut pork rind in water and salt for 30 minutes. On an oven pan, spread the cooked pork rind and bake at 300°F for 3 hours. Set aside and let cool.
   Deep fry rinds in a skillet in hot oil over high heat until they puff up.

Dipping Sauce

3 tablespoons apple cider
  vinegar
3 cloves crushed garlic
patis (see Glossary) or salt and freshly ground pepper to taste

Combine all ingredients and mix well.

Serves 6–8.

Pork Tapa • Marinated Pork Strips

2 pounds pork tenderloin, cut
  into quarter-inch slices
6 tablespoons soy sauce
6 tablespoons white vinegar
1 tablespoon finely minced garlic
1 tablespoon saltpeter
1 tablespoon salt
2 tablespoons sugar
2 tablespoons peanut oil

Combine all the ingredients and marinate overnight or for several days in the refrigerator. Drain pork and fry in oil until very well done. Drain on a piece of paper towel.

Serves 4–6

Empanaditas • Meat-Filled Turnovers

Pastry

1   14-ounce package of double-
    crust pastry (makes about 12 to
    16 four-inch squares).

Filling

1   tablespoon vegetable or corn
    oil
2   tablespoons minced garlic
¼   cup minced onion
¼   cup minced tomatoes
1   cup ground veal
1   cup ground pork
1   cup ground or chopped
    chicken
salt and freshly ground pepper to
    taste
1   cup chopped hard-boiled eggs
    (4 or 5 eggs)
1   cup chopped sweet pickles

Flatten pastry to a thickness of ⅛ inch. Cut into 4-inch squares. Set aside.

In a medium skillet, heat oil. Sauté garlic, onion and tomatoes. Cook until garlic is brown and onions turn transparent. Add veal, pork and chicken. Season with salt and pepper. Cook for 20 to 25 minutes, until meat is done. Add eggs and pickles. Cook for 5 minutes longer. Allow the mixture to cool.

Preheat oven to 400°F. Fill each piece of dough with a spoonful of the mixture. Fold to form a triangle. Wet the edges with water and seal. Arrange on a cookie sheet and bake the pastries for 25 to 30 minutes.

Serves 6–8.

Camaron Rebosado con Hamon
• Fried Shrimps with Ham

  1   pound large shrimps
  1   lemon
salt and freshly ground pepper
  2   eggs
 ½   cup cornstarch
  1   pound ham, thinly sliced in
       ¼-inch squares
  1   cup vegetable oil

Shell shrimps, leaving tail. Devein and cut the backs lengthwise. Squeeze lemon juice on shrimps. Add salt and pepper and set aside. Beat the eggs and add the cornstarch to make a thick batter. Place a strip of ham in each open shrimp, dip in batter and deep fry in the oil. Serve with pickled relish (see Chapter 11).

Serves 4–6.

Camaron Rebosado • Fried Shrimps

   1   pound shrimps
juice of 1 lemon
salt and freshly ground pepper
   2   eggs, beaten
   1   cup cornstarch
soy sauce and lemon juice to taste

Shell shrimps, leaving tail. Devein shrimps and split back in half, being careful not to separate halves. Marinate in lemon juice, salt and pepper for about 15 minutes.

    Dip shrimp in batter made from mixture of beaten eggs and cornstarch. Deep fry and drain on paper towel. Serve with soy sauce and lemon juice or Agre Dulce (see page 202).

Serves 4–6.

Relleno Alimasag • Stuffed Crabs

6   medium-large steamed crabs
2   tablespoons crushed garlic
½   cup chopped onion
1   medium-size tomato, chopped
2   eggs, separated
1   teaspoon salt
white pepper
3   tablespoons cooking oil (any
     light oil, such as safflower or
     soybean)

Remove the meat of the crabs from the shells. Set aside shells. Sauté garlic, onion, tomato and crabmeat.

Clean crab shells and stuff with sautéd crabmeat mixture. Beat egg whites 8 to 10 minutes, until stiff. Add the yolks, salt and pepper and beat 3 minutes. Place about a tablespoon of egg over stuffed crab. Fry in hot oil in open pan for 5 minutes on each side, or until slightly brown.

Serves 6.

Pinsec • Fried Wonton

½   pound finely chopped shrimps
¼   pound ground pork
1   six-ounce can crabmeat
¼   cup finely chopped green
        onion
dash of garlic powder
salt and freshly ground pepper
1   egg
¼   cup finely chopped water
      chestnuts
1   package wonton wrapper (sold
      in Oriental stores)
1   cup vegetable oil

Combine all ingredients except wonton wrapper and blend very well. Wrap about ½ teaspoon of filling in each wonton wrapper by folding one side to form a triangle. Seal with a few drops of water; set aside. Deep fry and drain on paper towel. Serve with plum sauce.

Plum Sauce

1   cup plum preserves
¼   cup white vinegar
1   tablespoon cornstarch
1   teaspoon cayenne pepper

Combine all ingredients and blend very well. Place in a saucepan and bring to a boil.

Serves 4–6.

Ukoy • Bean Sprout Fritters

Batter

- 2 eggs
- 1 cup cornstarch
- 1 tablespoon achuette juice (from anatto seeds, see page 204)

Filling

- 1 pound bean sprouts
- 12 medium-size shrimps, with shell
- 1 piece bean curd, cut into thin pieces
- ¼ pound ground pork

fat for frying (enough to cover fritters)
- ½ teaspoon bagoong

Beat the eggs very well; add the cornstarch and the juice of the achuette. In a saucer, place 2 tablespoons of the batter; arrange some bean sprouts, shrimp, bean curd, ground pork and ½ teaspoon of bagoong on top. Cover with 2 tablespoons of the batter and deep-fat fry. Serve hot with white vinegar, salt and crushed garlic, or with Sausawang Suka (see page 203).

Yield: 12 fritters.

Siomai • Boiled Dumplings

Wrapper

1 cup water
1 tablespoon vegetable or corn
   oil
¼ teaspoon salt
1½ cups all-purpose flour

Bring water, cooking oil and salt to a boil, then pour in flour. Remove from heat and beat until mixture forms a ball. Divide the dough into 1¼-inch balls. Roll each ball on a floured board until paper thin. Set aside.

Filling

1 cup shelled, deveined and
   chopped shrimp
¼ cup ground pork or beef
1 cup minced water chestnuts
¼ cup minced scallions
¼ cup minced onion
1 egg
1 teaspoon freshly ground
   pepper
1 teaspoon salt
soy sauce and lemon slice to
   garnish

Mix all the ingredients for the filling in a bowl. Spoon 1 tablespoon of the mixture into each wrapper. Fold and seal. Arrange in a steamer and steam for 30 minutes. Serve with soy sauce and lemon slices.

Serves 4–6.

Dilis Crisps • Anchovy Crisps

⅓ cup sugar
⅓ cup vinegar
1 teaspoon red hot sauce
½ teaspoon salt
⅛ ounce package of dried dilis
  (Filipino anchovies)
2 cups flours
½ cup oil (any light oil, such as
  safflower or soybean) for
  frying

In a medium bowl, mix sugar, vinegar, hot sauce and salt. Toss dilis in the mixture until well coated and dredge in flour. In a medium skillet, fry dilis over moderate heat until golden brown and crispy, keeping each one separate. Drain on paper towel. Serve with a dip of vinegar, salt and pepper.

Serves 4.

Chicken-Asparagus Soup

> 5 cups chicken broth
> salt and freshly ground pepper to
>   taste
> one 16-ounce can asparagus spears
> 3 tablespoons cornstarch
> ½ cup water
> 1 chicken breast, boned and
>   sliced, shredded just before
>   cooking
> 2 tablespoons minced cooked
>   ham

In a medium pot, combine chicken broth, salt and pepper. Add the liquid from the can of asparagus. Thicken the broth with cornstarch. Slice the asparagus spears into 1-inch lengths and add them to the broth. Add ½ cup water. Bring the whole mixture to a boil, then remove from heat. Add the chicken to the broth and bring back to a boil, stirring briskly. Cook until chicken is tender. Sprinkle with ham bits; serve hot.

Serves 4.

3

Rice Dishes

Throughout southeast Asia, from Japan to parts of Australia, cultivated rice constitutes the bulk of the people's diet. It is inconceivable for the Filipino, even for one who has resided in the United States or elsewhere for decades, to have a meal without rice. For rice enhances the flavor of many types of dishes and makes a meal more satisfying.

Rice has been part of the diet of the people of the Philippines for centuries. Today it can appear at any meal, in any course. For breakfast in some regions, soft young rice is eaten fresh (raw) with milk. More commonly last night's leftover rice is sautéed and served with sausages. At lunch, rice may be served fried with an endless variety of mixed vegetables and meats. For *merienda cena*, the favored mid-afternoon snack, sweet rice cakes (in many different forms) are favorites. For dinner, rice may be the basis for Arroz Valenciana, a dish of chicken, pork, shrimp and sausages cooked with tomatoes and saffron. The rice takes on the color of the saffron, the juice of the tomatoes and the flavor of all the ingredients.

Some recipes take their names from the places where they originated. Arroz a la Luzonia means rice cooked in the manner of the Filipinos from Luzon. Arroz a la Cubana is a recipe from Cuba in which the rice is served in individual cups, ringed with cooked meat and topped with fried bananas and fried eggs.

Some recipes are better at certain times of the year. On wintery evenings, people warm themselves with Arroz Caldo con Gotto, a steaming rice stew with tripe, and Arroz Caldo con Pollo, a hot rice stew with chicken.

Though there are many ways to cook rice, it is most often served simply plain and boiled. In this way it acts as an essential counterpoint to the sharp flavors of the other dishes. Rice in some form is a must at every Filipino meal. If you are serious about Filipino cooking in general, a rice cooker can make preparation easy.

In most places in the United States, rice is rice, and the distinctions between types of rice and their various qualities that are made in the Orient simply are not made here. However, it is possible to find short-grain, glutinous rice in Oriental grocery stores. This rice forms sticky clumps when it is cooked and is much better for dessert recipes. The long-grain rice found in most food markets is ideal as an accompaniment to the Filipino meal. However, care must be taken in cooking white rice to keep the grains together.

Kaning Puti • Boiled Rice

Tradition demands a thick steel pan for cooking rice. However, for convenience, an electric rice cooker is now a common substitute. Rice cookers imported from Japan are available in most department stores and Oriental food stores.

2 cups raw white rice
4 cups water
dash of salt

In a heavy saucepan, wash rice two or three times and drain. Add water and salt. Bring to a boil and simmer for about 15 minutes or until rice is cooked.

When using a rice cooker follow manufacturer's directions for timing.

Serves 4.

Sinangag • Philippine Fried Rice

- 4 tablespoons vegetable or corn oil
- 2 tablespoons minced garlic
- ¼ cup minced shallots
- 4 cups cold cooked rice (refrigerated leftover rice), mashed lightly with 1 cup water
- 1 tablespoon soy sauce
- 1 teaspoon salt
- ¼ teaspoon freshly ground pepper

In a 10-inch frying pan, heat oil and fry garlic till light brown. Add shallots, rice, soy sauce, salt and pepper. Stir the mixture constantly to prevent it from sticking to the pan and to ensure even cooking. Cook and continue stirring for 10 minutes. Serve hot.

Serves 6−8.

Shanghai Fried Rice
• Philippine Shanghai-Style Fried Rice

 2 tablespoons finely minced
    garlic
 ¼ cup finely minced shallots
 4 tablespoons vegetable or corn
    oil
 3 Chinese sausages, sliced into
    ⅛-inch-thick pieces
 ½ cup finely sliced pork loin
 ½ cup chopped fresh shrimps,
    shelled
 3 tablespoons soy sauce
 ¼ cup finely chopped parsley
 5 cups cold cooked rice
    (refrigerated leftover rice),
    mashed lightly with 1 cup of
    cold water
 ¼ cup scallions

In a 10- or 12-inch frying pan, fry garlic and shallots in oil. Add sausages, pork and shrimps. Season with soy sauce and parsley. Add rice. Continue frying and turning for 5 to 10 minutes, to blend all ingredients. When done, garnish with scallions.

Serves 8.

Arroz Caldo Con Pollo • Rice Chicken Soup

3   tablespoons vegetable or corn
     oil
2   tablespoons minced garlic
¼   cup chopped onion
8   ½-inch slices of ginger
1   2- to 3½-pound chicken, cut
     into serving pieces
4   tablespoons patis (see
     Glossary) or 2 tablespoons salt
6   cups water
2   cups uncooked rice
¼   cup chopped scallion
¼   teaspoon freshly ground
     pepper

In a large covered stockpot, heat oil and sauté garlic, onion and ginger. Wait for garlic to brown and onions to become transparent. Add the chicken and patis or salt. Cover and let simmer for 5 minutes. Chicken will produce its own juices. Add water and rice. Stirring often to prevent sticking, simmer for 25 minutes over low heat or until chicken and rice are tender. Add chopped scallion and pepper before serving.

Serves 6–8.

Arroz Caldo con Goto • Rice Soup with Tripe

- 2 pounds tripe (3 cups, cut into bite-size pieces)
- 8 cups water
- 5 tablespoons vegetable or corn oil
- 2 tablespoons minced garlic
- 1 large onion, diced
- 1½ cups uncooked rice
- 1½ tablespoons salt or patis (see Glossary)
- 2 tablespoons garlic, minced and fried till brown
- ¼ cup finely chopped scallion
- ¼ teaspoon freshly ground pepper

In a stockpot, bring tripe to a boil in 8 cups water, then reduce heat and simmer until tender (about 3 hours). Add more water if needed to prevent sticking. Drain tripe, reserving 6 cups broth, and set aside. In another pot, heat 3 tablespoons oil and sauté garlic and onion. Garlic is done when light brown and onions when transparent. Add rice and sauté for 5 minutes. Add reserved broth in which the tripe was cooked. Bring mixture to a boil, stirring occasionally. Reduce heat to simmer and continue cooking for another 30 minutes or until rice is done.

While waiting for rice to cook, heat 2 tablespoons of oil in a skillet and fry 2 tablespoons of garlic until golden brown. Set aside. When the rice is finally cooked, add the tripe and the salt or patis and continue cooking on low fire for another 3 to 5 minutes. Serve in soup bowls. Sprinkle fried finely minced garlic with chopped scallion and pepper on top.

Serves 4.

Arroz a la Luzonia or Biringe • Luzon-Style Rice

3 tablespoons vegetable or corn oil
2 tablespoons minced garlic
½ cup chopped onion
1 3-pound chicken, boiled and cut into serving pieces
1 cup shrimp, shelled and deveined
1 cup pork, boiled for 15 minutes, then cut into ½-inch cubes
1 cup ham, cubed into ¼-inch pieces
1 piece chorizo de Bilbao or pepperoni, sliced into ⅛-inch pieces

2 cups uncooked rice, washed and drained (glutinous rice is preferable)
1 bay leaf
2 tablespoons salt
2 twelve-ounce cans coconut milk (available in Oriental stores)
⅛ teaspoon paprika
1 cup sweet peas
3 hard-boiled eggs, sliced

In a stockpot, heat oil and sauté garlic until brown and onion until transparent. Add chicken, shrimp, pork, ham, chorizos de Bilbao or pepperoni and bring to a boil. Add rice, bay leaf, salt, coconut milk and paprika. Stir mixture to prevent it from sticking to bottom of pan. Lower heat, cover and simmer till meat and rice are tender. This takes about 20 to 30 minutes. Add peas and cook for another 3 minutes. Garnish with hard-boiled eggs.

Serves 4–6.

Arroz a la Valenciana • Valencia-Style Rice

A simple adaptation of the Spanish paella, without the seafood ingredients.

1	2½- to 3-pound chicken, cut into serving pieces
½	pound pork loin, cut into ½-inch strips
½	teaspoon salt
½	teaspoon pepper
½	cup corn or vegetable oil
2	teaspoons anatto seeds or 1 teaspoon paprika
1	tablespoon finely minced garlic
1	cup chopped onion
1	cup tomato sauce
6	potatoes, peeled and quartered
2	pieces pepperoni, sliced into ⅛-inch-thick pieces

4	cups water
½	cup red bell peppers with the seeds removed and sliced lengthwise into ½-inch-wide strips
2	cups sweet peas
3	cups rice, boiled in 3 cups water and 2 cups coconut milk (available in Oriental Stores), or in 5 cups water
½	cup pimento-stuffed green olives
3	hard-boiled eggs, sliced crosswise

Season chicken and pork with salt and pepper. Fry in oil in a stockpot until brown. Set aside the chicken and pork pieces. In the same stockpot, fry the anatto seeds in the remaining oil to give a golden-orange color, then discard seeds. Sauté garlic, onion and tomato sauce until mixture has taken on a saucelike consistency. Add potatoes, pepperoni and 4 cups of water. Cover and bring to a boil. Stir and reduce heat to low. Add bell pepper and sweet peas. When the bell pepper and peas lose their crispness, remove 1 cup of stock from the pot and set aside. Add cooked rice, fried pork and chicken to the stockpot. Mix thoroughly until well blended. Add reserved stock and cook uncovered over low heat until mixture becomes dry. Serve on a large platter and garnish with pimento-stuffed green olives and sliced hard-boiled eggs.

Serves 6–8.

Philippine - Style Paella

1 2-pound fryer chicken, cut into pieces
1 2-pound pork tenderloin
1 pound large shrimps
salt and pepper to taste
3 large crabs
20 fresh littleneck clams
6 cups water
½ cup olive oil
½ teaspoon paprika
2 tablespoons chopped garlic
¼ cup chopped onion
2 chorizos de Bilbao or pepperonis, sliced thin
3 cups raw rice (glutinous or sticky rice if available)
½ cup tomato sauce
1 small bay leaf
1 green bell pepper, sliced into 1-inch pieces
¼ teaspoon saffron mixed with 1 teaspoon water (optional)
1 cup frozen peas
2 pieces pimento cut into 1-inch squares
2 hard-boiled eggs

Cut chicken and pork into 1½-inch pieces. Shell shrimps leaving tails; slit and remove black veins; dredge with salt and pepper.

Boil crabs and quarter. Crack shells of crab claws and set aside.

Boil clams in 6 cups water until they open. Remove empty top shells and set aside. Reserve 6 cups clam broth.

Preheat oven to 350°F. Heat olive oil in a large pan and add chicken, pork, paprika, garlic, onion and chorizo or pepperoni. Toss for a few minutes and add rice. Stir until rice is slightly brown. Add tomato sauce, clam broth, bay leaf, salt and pepper and stir for a few minutes. Add shrimps and bell peppers and saffron if used. Bring to a boil.

Transfer to a serving casserole and bake covered at 350°F for 30 minutes. Uncover the casserole and arrange clams, crabs, peas and pimento on top. Cover and cook for 5 minutes. Decorate top with slices of hard-boiled eggs before serving.

Serves 12–15.

Arroz a la Cubana • Cuban-Style Rice

3	tablespoons vegetable or corn oil	¼	cup raisins
1	tablespoon minced garlic	½	teaspoon salt
¼	cup minced shallots	¼	teaspoon pepper
½	cup diced tomatoes	½	cup sweet peas
½	pound ground beef	5	tablespoons peanut oil
½	pound ground pork	3	ripe plantain bananas, sliced
3	tablespoons soy sauce	5	eggs
		5	cups cooked rice

In a large stockpot, heat 3 tablespoons oil and sauté garlic until light brown. Add shallots and cook until transparent. Add tomatoes and cook for 5 minutes. Stir in ground beef, pork and soy sauce. Cook until meat is brown. Add raisins, salt and pepper and stir constantly. Add peas and simmer for another 5 minutes.

In a separate skillet, heat 3 tablespoons peanut oil and fry plantain slices. Remove from heat and set aside. Put 2 more tablespoons peanut oil in the pan and fry 5 eggs sunny-side up. Set aside.

In a large serving platter, arrange cooked rice with meat in the center. Top with fried eggs and surround side of platter with fried bananas.

Serves 8.

4

Adobos—Variations and Other Stews

If the Philippines had a national dish, it would have to be *adobo*. Though adobo is not only a dish but a style of cooking, what most people think of when they hear the word is a stew with the basic elements of chicken and pork in a sauce of soy sauce, white vinegar, garlic and peppercorns. The variations are endless, and whether served dry or moist, whole or shredded, the subtle sourness that makes the dish unique is always present.

Almost anything can be cooked adobo-style: beef, fish, shellfish and vegetables, in addition to pork or chicken, are excellent. Squid adobo-style is an eating experience not to be missed.

Adobo has become one of the most popular dishes in the Philippines because of its flavor, of course, but also because the cooking process (in vinegar) is a preservation process. The finished dish will keep for four or five days without refrigeration—a blessing in the tropics.

Served with white rice and a cold San Miguel (the national beer), the dish can be eaten often.

Adobong Manok ● Chicken Adobo

- 1 3-pound chicken, cut into serving pieces
- ½ cup soy sauce
- ¾ cup white vinegar
- 1 or 2 heads of garlic, crushed
- 2 bay leaves
- ½ tablespoon peppercorns
- salt to taste

Bring to a boil the chicken together with the soy sauce, vinegar, garlic, bay leaves and peppercorns and simmer for half an hour. Remove the chicken pieces from the pot and broil them in a pan for 10 minutes. Let the sauce in the pot boil until it is reduced by half. Add salt to taste. Cover the broiled chicken pieces with the sauce. Serve hot.

Serves 6.

Adobong Baboy • Pork Adobo

1   pound pork loin, cut into
    chunks
1   head of garlic, crushed
¼   cup soy sauce
1   teaspoon freshly ground
    black pepper
½   cup white vinegar
1   tablespoon vegetable or corn oil

Place the pork in a medium-size pot together with the garlic, soy sauce, pepper and vinegar and let stand for 2 hours. Cook slowly in the same pot until the pork is tender (about 30 minutes). Transfer the pieces of garlic from the pot to a separate pan and fry in hot oil until brown. Add the pork pieces to the garlic and then fry until brown. Drain. Add the broth to the fried pork and garlic and simmer for 10 minutes.

Serves 2–4.

Adobong Hipon Sa Gata
● Shrimp Adobo in Coconut Milk

½   cup white vinegar
¼   cup water
⅛   teaspoon freshly ground
       pepper
1   tablespoon finely minced garlic
patis or salt to taste
1   pound large fresh shrimps,
       unshelled
2   twelve-ounce cans coconut
       milk

In a medium-size stockpot, prepare the marinade (vinegar, water, pepper, garlic and patis or salt). Add shrimps and let stand for 1 hour. Cook in the same pot with the lid off, turning the shrimps often, until the pot is almost dry. Stir in the coconut milk and allow the sauce to thicken. This takes about 20 minutes.

Serves 2.

Adobong Kangkong • Vegetable Adobo

2 pounds kangkong (see Glossary) or spinach
½ tablespoon finely minced garlic
½ cup vegetable or corn oil
1 tablespoon lemon or lime juice
3 tablespoons soy sauce
½ tablespoon salt
freshly ground pepper to taste

Wash and sort kangkong or spinach. Separate leaves and cut stems into 1-inch lengths. Sauté the garlic in oil, and when it is golden brown, add the kangkong, lemon or lime juice, soy sauce and salt. Cover and bring to a boil. Add freshly ground pepper to taste. Serve hot.

Serves 4.

Adobong Isda • Fish Adobo

3 pounds trout, bluefish or
  similar fish, dressed
1 tablespoon finely minced garlic
⅓ cup apple cider vinegar
¼ cup water
1 tablespoon salt

¼ teaspoon freshly ground
  pepper
1 small bay leaf (optional)
3 tablespoons vegetable or corn
  oil

Combine all ingredients in a saucepan except the oil. Marinate for one hour. Bring to a boil. Cover and simmer for 5 minutes. Remove fish and set aside. Reduce sauce to half and set aside. Fry fish in hot oil till it is brown, and pour sauce in with fish. Simmer for 3 minutes and serve hot.

Serves 4.

Adobong Hito • Catfish Adobo

2 pounds catfish
2 tablespoons finely minced
  ginger
1 tablespoon finely minced garlic
1 cup white vinegar

salt and freshly ground pepper to
  taste
4 tablespoons vegetable or corn
  oil

Marinate fish in ginger, garlic, vinegar, salt and pepper for 3 hours. Take the garlic bits from the marinade and fry in oil until golden brown. Add the fish and the marinade. Bring to a boil and simmer for 10 minutes, turning fish several times.

Serves 4.

Adobong Talong • Eggplant Adobo

4 cups eggplant, cut into
  2-by-2-inch pieces
¼ cup vegetable or corn oil
½ cup white vinegar
¼ cup soy sauce
1 tablespoon finely minced garlic

Fry eggplant cubes in oil until brown. Set aside on paper towel to absorb the oil. In a saucepan, bring vinegar, soy sauce and garlic to a boil and simmer for 6 minutes. Add fried eggplant to mixture and cook for 5 minutes more, turning eggplant slices several times. Serve hot.

Serves 4.

Tulyang Inadobo • Clam or Mussel Adobo

2 cups littleneck clams, shelled
1 tablespoon finely minced garlic
3 tablespoons white vinegar
½ teaspoon peppercorns
1 cup water
2 tablespoons vegetable or corn
  oil
patis or salt to taste

In a 4-quart stockpot, boil shelled clams in garlic, vinegar, peppercorns and water. Set aside the broth. Remove clams from the pot and fry in oil until brown. Pour broth back in with the clams and simmer for 10 minutes. Add salt or patis to taste. Serve hot.

Serves 4–6.

Adobong Manok Sa Gata
• Chicken Adobo in Coconut Milk

1	3-pound chicken, cut in serving pieces
1½	cups apple cider vinegar
6	tablespoons finely minced garlic
½	cup soy sauce
1	teaspoon freshly ground black pepper
2	bay leaves (optional)
1	tablespoon peppercorns
1	tablespoon brown sugar (optional)
1	12-ounce can coconut milk

patis or salt to taste

Combine all ingredients in a saucepan and marinate for two hours. Boil mixture till chicken is tender. Separate sauce from chicken and broil chicken till brown. Reduce the sauce over moderate heat to half and pour over chicken.

Serves 4–6.

Adobong Karne Sa Gata
• Beef Stewed in Coconut Milk

3	pounds cubed stewing beef (chuck)
¾	cup white vinegar
1	head of garlic, crushed
½	cup soy sauce
4	bay leaves
1½	tablespoons whole peppercorns
1	tablespoon freshly ground pepper
1	tablespoon sugar
4	tablespoons vegetable or corn oil
1	tablespoon patis or salt
1	12-ounce can coconut milk

Combine the beef, vinegar, garlic, soy sauce, bay leaves, peppercorns, ground pepper and sugar in a saucepan. Let stand for 2 hours. Bring mixture to a boil and simmer about an hour or until meat is tender.

Heat the oil in a skillet and add the garlic from cooked mixture. Cook until brown. Add the meat and cook, stirring, until it is browned on all sides. Add patis or salt to taste and the coconut milk and the sauce and simmer for about 5 minutes.

Serves 4.

Adobong Labong • Bamboo Shoots Adobo

5	tablespoons vegetable or corn oil
1	tablespoon minced garlic
¼	cup minced onion
½	cup pork, boiled for 15 minutes and cut into ½-inch cubes (save 1 cup stock)
½	cup shelled, deveined and minced shrimps
1½	tablespoons patis or salt
1	cup reserved pork stock
3	cups bamboo shoots cut into 2-by-2-inch squares
4	tablespoons white vinegar
	salt and freshly ground pepper to taste

Heat 2 tablespoons oil in a skillet and sauté garlic until light brown and onion until transparent. Stir in pork and shrimps and cook until shrimps are done (when they are pink). Add patis or salt, stock and bamboo shoots. Simmer for 15 minutes. Add vinegar. Continue simmering until the liquid has been reduced by half. Add remaining 3 tablespoons of oil and cook for another 10 minutes. Add salt and pepper to taste.

Serves 4.

Adobong Pusit • Squid Adobo

1 pound medium-size squid	1 cup water
½ cup white vinegar	2 tablespoons vegetable or corn
1 head garlic, minced	oil
freshly ground pepper to taste	¼ cup chopped onion
¼ cup soy sauce or salt	2 cups cubed red, ripe tomatoes

Wash and clean the squid thoroughly, removing the cuttle. Put squid in a saucepan (not aluminum) with the vinegar, garlic, pepper, soy sauce or salt and water. Cook over low heat until squid is tender, making sure it does not get overcooked and rubbery. Drain and set aside the squid broth.

Heat oil in another saucepan and sauté the cooked garlic until brown, onion until transparent and tomatoes until soft. Add the squid and simmer for 3 minutes. Pour squid broth over mixture and bring to a boil. Serve hot.

Serves 4.

Adobong Okra • Okra Adobo

20 pieces young okra	4 tablespoons lemon or lime
2 tablespoons vegetable or corn	juice
oil	3 tablespoons soy sauce
½ tablespoon finely minced garlic	salt and pepper to taste
1 cup finely minced onion	

Wash and parboil okra for 5 minutes. Drain. In a skillet, heat oil and sauté okra, garlic and onions until garlic is brown and onions are transparent. Add lemon or lime juice and soy sauce. Simmer for 6 to 8 minutes or until okra is tender. Add salt and pepper to taste.

Serves 4.

5

Poultry Dishes

The Filipino taste appreciates the mingling of many different spices and seasonings, and chicken is perfect for absorbing various flavors. So it is little wonder that chicken is a favorite in the Philippines.

Chicken dishes range from full-flavor creations to subtle-flavor dishes. The most popular marinade for chicken imparts a distinct taste; soy sauce, patis (fish sauce), lemon juice and pepper are used. Nilagang Manok—boiled chicken—is a mild-tasting everyday meal.

Chicken dishes also range from very complex to easy-to-prepare ones. Chicken Relleno requires hours of preparation but is well worth the effort. Chicken Tinola is easy to prepare and especially delicious even when American substitutes are used.

Ginataang Manok
• Chicken Cooked in Coconut Milk

1   2- to 3-pound chicken, cut into
    serving pieces
¼   cup white vinegar
3   cloves garlic, crushed
½   cup water
1   12-ounce can coconut milk
1   tablespoon salt
¼   teaspoon pepper

In a saucepan, combine all ingredients. Bring to a boil and simmer about 20 minutes until practically all the liquid has evaporated and a thick sauce remains. Serve hot.

Serves 4.

Chicken Pastel • Chicken Pie

1 2-pound chicken, cut into serving pieces	1 tablespoon white wine
3 tablespoons soy sauce	1 diced carrot
juice of 1 lemon	1½ cups diced potatoes
1 cup margarine	1 14-ounce can Vienna sausage, strained and diced
¼ cup finely minced onion	¾ cup green olives
1 cup mushrooms, sliced in half	½ cup sweet peas
1 pepperoni, sliced into pieces ⅛-inch thick	¼ cup grated Parmesan cheese
2 cups chicken broth	salt and pepper to taste
	1 beaten egg

Marinate chicken in soy sauce and lemon for about 1 hour. Heat margarine in a large skillet. Brown chicken pieces. Remove the chicken and set aside. In the same skillet, sauté onion, mushrooms and pepperoni. Add the chicken, broth and wine. Simmer over low heat until chicken is tender. Add carrots, potatoes, Vienna sausage, olives, sweet peas and grated cheese. Cook for 10 minutes longer. Season with salt and pepper. Transfer the whole mixture to a greased pie plate; reserve whatever is left over to eat separately.

Pastry Crust

2 cups flour	½ cup vegetable or corn oil
1 teaspoon salt	¼ cup cold water

Preheat oven to 450°F. Combine flour and salt in a bowl. Make a well in the center and add the oil and cold water. Stir and mix lightly into a ball. On a flat surface, roll out the pastry and shape it. Cover the mixture in the pie plate with it, pressing the edges to seal the top. Prick the pastry with a fork to let off steam. Brush the outside of the pastry with a beaten egg and bake for 15 minutes or until golden brown. Serve hot.

Serves 8.

Apritadang Manok • Chicken Apritada-Style

1 2- to 3-pound chicken
1 clove garlic, crushed
¼ cup chopped onion
1 6-ounce can tomato sauce
1 bay leaf
1 tablespoon peppercorns

2 teaspoons salt
1 teaspoon pepper
¼ cup water
2 medium size potatoes, cut in cubes
1 4-ounce can pimentos

Cut chicken into serving pieces. Simmer for 15 minutes in garlic, onion, tomato sauce, bay leaf, peppercorns, salt, pepper and water. Add cubed potatoes and pimento. Continue to cook until the potatoes are tender. Serve hot.

Serves 4.

Rellenong Manok • Baked Stuffed Chicken

1   whole 2- to 3-pound chicken,
    boned (be careful not to pierce
    the skin)

Marinade

3   tablespoons soy sauce
1   tablespoon sugar
2   tablespoons lemon

Combine all ingredients and marinate boned chicken for 3 hours.

Stuffing

½   pound ground ham
½   pound ground pork
½   pound ground chicken
¼   pound frankfurters, finely minced
1½ ounces raisins
1   tablespoon lemon juice
2   tablespoons soy sauce
1   tablespoon garlic powder
2   tablespoons bread crumbs
¼   cup chopped onion
5   ounces sweet relish (canned)
2   raw eggs
2   teaspoons pepper
salt to taste
3   hard-boiled eggs, peeled
4   ounces melted butter or margarine, for baking
2   pieces hot sausage (pepperoni
    or Polish sausage), sliced
    lengthwise into quarters

Combine all the ingredients for stuffing except hard-boiled eggs, melted butter and hot sausages and mix well. Stuff the chicken with the mixture and the 3 hard-boiled eggs and hot sausages, taking care to arrange the eggs and sausages inside the chicken longitudinally (from neck to tail). Sew the slits at the neck and the tail of the bird. Place the chicken in a baking dish and brush with the melted butter. Wrap in aluminum foil. Preheat the oven to 350°F. Bake for 1 hour. Remove aluminum-foil wrapper and continue baking until chicken is golden brown. Serve with sauce.

Sauce

drippings from chicken
  2 tablespoons flour
  2 tablespoons soy sauce
  1 tablespoon finely minced garlic
  2 tablespoons vegetable or corn
     oil
salt to taste

Collect drippings from the baking dish. Add 2 tablespoons flour and one table-spoon soy sauce. Set aside.

In a small saucepan, sauté garlic in oil until brown. Add the mixture of flour, soy sauce and drippings. Season with salt. Cook about 5 minutes, stirring often. Slice chicken and serve with sauce.

Serves 8.

Pocherong Manok
• Chicken Pochero-Style

one 2- to 3-pound chicken
  1 chorizo de Bilbao or pepperoni
 10 peppercorns
salt to taste
  2 plantain bananas
  2 small potatoes, quartered
 ½ small green cabbage, quartered
 ½ small head bak choy (Chinese
      vegetable), cut into 2-inch
      slices
  2 tablespoons vegetable oil
  1 clove garlic, crushed
  1 small onion, diced
 8-ounce can tomato sauce
 ½ cup water
 8-ounce can chick peas

Stew chicken in enough water to cook. Add sausage, peppercorns and salt and cook until done. Drain the juice and set aside.

Boil plantains separately (10 minutes if green, 5 minutes if ripe). Peel after cooking and set aside.

Using the drained juice of the chicken, cook potatoes until done; add the cabbage and bak choy and set aside.

Sauté the garlic, onion, tomato sauce, chicken and sausage in the 2 tablespoons of oil. Add ½ cup water and chick peas and continue to cook for about 10 minutes. Serve chicken with cabbage, bak choy, potatoes and bananas.

Serves 4−6.

Sinigang Na Manok
• Boiled Chicken with Vegetables # 1

one 2-pound chicken, cut into
      serving pieces
 ½ cup sliced tomatoes
 ¼ cup sliced onion
juice of 1 lemon
  1 cup green beans, cut into
      2-inch pieces
  1 cup small radishes, quartered
  1 small bunch of green leafy
      vegetable (broccoli, spinach,
      rabe or collard greens)
  1 tablespoon salt or patis

Boil chicken, tomatoes, onion and lemon juice in enough water to cover chicken. Cook until chicken is almost tender. Add the rest of the ingredients and continue cooking until chicken is tender and vegetables are just crisp-tender. Serve hot.

Serves 4.

Pesang Manok
• Boiled Chicken with Vegetables # 2

1	2- to 3-pound chicken, cut into serving pieces
½	onion, cut into wedges
2	medium-size potatoes
1	tablespoon peppercorns
1	teaspoon salt
½	small green cabbage
1	head bak choy (Chinese vegetable)
1	bunch chopped scallions

Boil chicken in enough water to cover, with onion, potatoes, peppercorns and salt. When chicken is tender, add the cabbage, bak choy and scallions. Cook until vegetables are crisp-tender. Serve hot.

Serves 4.

Misuang Manok • Chicken with Noodles

2	tablespoons crushed garlic
3	tablespoons cooking oil
¼	cup sliced onion
one	2-pound chicken, cut into serving pieces
2	tablespoons patis or 1 tablespoon salt
¼	teaspoon pepper
6	cups water
2	packs misua (threadlike noodles) or vermicelli
¼	cup scallions or green onions

Sauté garlic in oil until brown. Add onion, chicken, patis or salt and pepper. Cover, bring to a boil and simmer for 10 minutes. Add water, bring to a boil and simmer until chicken is cooked. Add misua noodles and cook for another 5 minutes. Sprinkle with scallions before serving. Serve hot.

Serves 4.

Binakol • Chicken Soup with Coconut

6 cloves garlic, crushed
1 medium-size onion, chopped
5 ½-inch slices ginger
3 tablespoons vegetable oil
1 tablespoon salt and pepper to
   taste
1 2-pound chicken, boned and
   cut into 1-inch squares
6 cups chicken stock (made from
   chicken bones)
1 coconut, preferably a buko (see
   Glossary); meat cut into 1-inch
   squares (save juice)

Sauté garlic, onion and ginger in oil. Add salt and pepper. Add chicken and stir.
Pour in chicken stock. Simmer for 30 minutes or until chicken is tender. Add
coconut juice and meat. Season with more salt and pepper to taste.

Serves 6.

Tinolang Manok • Boiled Chicken with Ginger

2	tablespoons vegetable or corn oil
1½	tablespoons finely minced garlic
¼	cup finely minced onion
1	tablespoon peeled and minced ginger root
1	2- to 3-pound chicken, cut into serving pieces

salt and freshly ground pepper to taste

2	tablespoons patis or salt
3	cups water
2	cups cubed green papaya or zucchini
2	cups spinach leaves

In a large saucepan, heat oil. Sauté garlic, onion and ginger. Brown garlic and cook onion until transparent. Add chicken pieces and stir well until chicken is partly cooked. Season with salt, pepper and patis if desired. Add water. Cover and simmer over moderate heat until chicken is tender. Uncover pot and add papaya or zucchini. Cook until tender. Turn off heat and add spinach leaves. Serve hot.

Serves 4.

Linaga • Boiled Chicken Stew

- 1 3-pound chicken, cut into serving pieces
- 5 cups water
- 1 tablespoon ginger
- ½ teaspoon crushed peppercorns
- 2 teaspoons salt
- 2 cups quartered onion
- 1 cup celery cut into 2-inch lengths
- 4 medium potatoes, quartered
- 1 small cabbage, quartered
- ½ cup scallion cut into 2-inch lengths

In a large saucepan, combine chicken pieces, water, ginger, peppercorns, salt, onion and celery. Bring to a boil. Lower heat, cover and simmer until chicken is tender. Add potatoes. Simmer until tender. Add cabbage and green onions and cook until soft. Serve hot.

Serves 6.

Asadong Manok # 1 • Marinated Chicken Stew

1   2-pound chicken, cut into
    serving pieces

Marinade

¼   cup soy sauce
4   tablespoons lemon juice
½   cup water
½   teaspoon salt
3   tablespoons Worcestershire
    sauce
2   tablespoons cornstarch
    dissolved in a little water

Combine all the marinade ingredients, and marinate the chicken in the mixture for an hour in a large pot. Cover the pot and simmer gently for an hour until meat is tender. Serve hot.

Serves 4.

Asadong Manok # 2 • Sour Chicken Stew

½   cup red wine vinegar
½   cup water
2   tablespoons minced garlic
1   teaspoon salt
½   teaspoon pepper
1   2½-pound chicken, cut into
    serving pieces
¼   cup chopped onion
½   cup cubed red, ripe tomatoes
½   cup finely chopped chicken
    liver
2   teaspoons patis or salt

Mix vinegar, water, garlic, salt and pepper in a pot. Add chicken pieces, bring to a boil and simmer until chicken is tender. Add onion and tomatoes. Add the chicken liver. Simmer for another 10 minutes. Season with patis or salt before serving. Serve hot.

Serves 4.

Asadong Manok # 3 • Piquant Chicken Stew

  3   tablespoons vegetable or corn
      oil
  2   tablespoons crushed garlic
  ½   cup minced onion
  1   cup cubed red, ripe tomatoes
  1   3- to 4-pound chicken, cut into
      serving pieces
  1   tablespoon peppercorns or
      chili peppers
  ⅛   teaspoon freshly ground
      pepper
  2   bay leaves
  ¼   cup vinegar
  1   tablespoon paprika
  1   cup water
salt to taste

In a medium-size saucepan, heat oil and sauté garlic until light brown; add onion and wait until transparent before putting in tomatoes. When tomatoes turn soft, add chicken, peppercorns or chili peppers, ground pepper, bay leaves, vinegar, paprika, water and salt. Lower heat and simmer until meat is tender.

Serves 6–8.

Pritong Manok • Fried Chicken Philippine-Style

    1   2- to 3-pound chicken, cut into
        serving pieces
    ¼   cup white vinegar
    1   cup water
    4   cloves garlic, crushed
salt and pepper to taste
    1   cup cooking oil

Simmer chicken in vinegar, water, garlic, salt and pepper until almost done.
Drain off liquid. Deep fry chicken in oil until brown. Drain chicken.

Serves 3–4.

Pinatisang Manok • Chicken with Patis

    2   cloves garlic, crushed
    ¼   cup diced onion
    1   tablespoon diced fresh ginger
    1   2- to 3-pound chicken, cut into
        serving pieces
    3   cups rice water*
 2¼   cups patis (see Glossary)
    ½   cup water
fresh vegetable leaves (spinach or
        watercress)

Sauté garlic, onion and ginger. Add cut-up chicken and season with patis and ½
cup water. Simmer until chicken is almost done. Add rice water and fresh leaves
and continue to cook until chicken is tender. Serve hot.

Serves 4.

---

*Mix 3 cups of water with 2 cups of rice. Drain off the liquid—this is rice water.

Gallina con Guisantes • Chicken with Sweet Peas

- 2 cups flour
- 1 teaspoon salt
- ¼ teaspoon pepper
- 1 2- to 3-pound chicken, cut into serving pieces
- ½ cup butter
- ¼ cup cooking oil
- 2 carrots, cut into 1½-inch pieces
- 1 bay leaf
- ¼ teaspoon oregano
- 1 bunch leeks, chopped
- 4 cups chicken or beef broth
- 3 potatoes, quartered
- 1 cup green peas (frozen or canned)

Mix flour, salt and pepper in a plastic bag. Drop chicken pieces into bag and shake to coat each piece. Melt butter and heat oil in a skillet. Fry coated chicken in butter-oil mixture until golden brown. Add carrots, bay leaf, oregano and leeks. Add chicken or beef broth and cook until chicken is almost tender. Add potatoes and green peas and continue to cook until chicken, potatoes and peas are tender. Serve hot.

Serves 4.

Talunang Manok • Defeated Chicken

The national sport in the Philippines is cockfighting. Cocks that have lost their last fight are called *talunan*. Because they were bred for the pit and not for the table, these roosters are tough. This special recipe is needed to make them tender. You can use stewing chicken as a substitute.

2	cups salted black beans
1	cup white vinegar
½	cup brown sugar
1	4- to 5-pound stewing fowl, cut into serving pieces
2	pounds pigs' feet
4	cups water
3	garlic heads, crushed
1	bay leaf
1	tablespoon oregano
1	small piece star anise
1	cinnamon stick

Mash beans with vinegar and brown sugar and place, with the chicken, pigs' feet and water, in a large pot. Boil until chicken and pigs' feet are tender (a pressure cooker may be used). Add garlic and spices to stock. Simmer until thick.

Serves 4–6.

Fried Pigeon

½ cup soy sauce
1 cup water
1 tablespoon sherry
1 tablespoon sugar
2 bay leaves
2 pigeons or squabs, dressed
1 tablespoon honey
cooking oil for deep frying
¼ lemon, sliced

Combine soy sauce, water, sherry, sugar and bay leaves and bring to a boil. Add pigeons and cook for 15 minutes, turning pigeons occasionally. Remove and cool. Rub with honey and let stand for 15 minutes.

Deep fry pigeons in a strainer or frying basket. Drain and chop pigeons into serving pieces and arrange on a platter. Garnish with lemon slices and serve with pepper-salt mixture.

Pepper-Salt Mixture

1 tablespoon salt
2 tablespoons pepper

Toss 1 tablespoon salt in a hot, dry saucepan for about 2 minutes. Add 2 tablespoons black pepper. Cook until extremely hot and smoking. Serve with fried pigeon.

Serves 2.

Pato Tim • Marinated Duck

Filipinos don't eat duck often, because it might lessen the supply of the very popular *balut*, a boiled egg in which the embryonic duck has just formed—it is a delicacy that is an acquired taste. When mature ducks are prepared for the table, this is the recipe that is usually used.

    1   medium-size duck, cut into
        serving pieces
    ¼   cup soy sauce
juice of 1 lemon
    4   tablespoons sherry
        small piece ginger, crushed
    ½   cup cooking oil
    1   6-ounce can asparagus or
        8 stalks fresh asparagus
    ½   pound fresh mushrooms,
        sliced
    ¼   cup water
    2   tablespoons cornstarch
salt (optional)

Clean duck very well. Marinate overnight in soy sauce, lemon juice, sherry and ginger.

Preheat oven to 350°F. Brown duck in hot cooking oil. Place duck in foil with asparagus and sliced mushrooms and bake for half-hour.

Combine the water from the asparagus and the ¼ cup water; add drippings from the baked duck. Blend together and thicken with cornstarch. Season with salt if desired. Pour sauce over duck and serve hot with rice.

Serves 5.

6
Pork Dishes

The supreme pork dish is Lechón, a whole roast suckling pig. The sight of a whole pig roasting over glowing coals will invariably start gastric juices flowing, and when it is served with the traditional sauce made of liver and pickled papaya, the dish becomes a gustatory treat that has no rival.

Originally the dish was prepared only for special occasions or fiestas, in the rural areas. In the 1800s, city elite and government officials of the Philippine Commonwealth gave the dish glamour by serving it at official functions. Now it is standard party fare. A simplified, easier-to-manage version of Lechón calls for using pork shoulder or pork loin, with the skin intact.

Another popular dish is barbecued pork. Barbecueing was introduced by the Americans, but there is a story that explains its Philippine transformation. An old gentleman raised in the Spanish tradition was curious about a barbecue pit that had been installed at a neighbor's home. He went to investigate while it was in use one day and was offered cubes of pork that had been cooked in it. As he ate, his expression showed that something was missing—the taste was not right. He then asked for a saucer of vinegar and crushed garlic and dipped a pork cube in it. When he tasted this, his face lit up with delight. Barbecued pork had gone native!

Other pork dishes have been greatly influenced by Spanish methods of cooking. Many of these are stews with familiar ingredients including tomatoes, garlic, onions, vinegar and soy sauce.

Asadong Baboy • Pork Chinese-Style

2 pounds pork loin

Marinade

1 cup water
⅓ cup soy sauce
⅓ cup brown sugar
2 tablespoons white wine
½ teaspoon salt
2 tablespoons finely minced
garlic

Marinate the whole pork loin for 30 minutes or more in a large pot. Cover the pot and bring the mixture to a boil. Lower heat and simmer until meat is tender (about 30 minutes). Serve hot with the marinade.

Serves 6.

Lechón • Roast Pork

3- to 4-pound pork shoulder, with
    skin
 3 teaspoons salt
 1 cup freshly ground pepper

Season meat with salt and pepper. Bake at 350° F for about 2 hours or until skin is brown and crisp. Serve with Lechón Sauce.

Lechón Sauce or Liver Sauce

½ pound chicken liver or 1 cup
    liver pâté
½ cup apple cider vinegar
 1 cup bread crumbs
 3 tablespoons finely minced
    garlic
 1 cup finely minced onion
salt and freshly ground pepper to
    taste
 3 tablespoons brown sugar

In a saucepan, combine all the sauce ingredients and bring the mixture to a long simmer (about 20 minutes) over moderate heat. If using chicken liver, broil the liver till it is half done first and extract the juices by pressing through a sieve or strainer.

Serves 8.

Lechón Kawali • Pan-Fried Roast Pork

2- to 3-pound pork shoulder, with
    skin
  4 cups water
  2 tablespoons salt
1 to 2 cups cooking oil
  2 cups Lechón Sauce (see
    page 86)

Boil pork in water with salt until skin is tender. Remove from heat and drain. Cool and air dry. Deep fry in oil until tiny blisters appear on the skin. Chop into serving pieces. Serve with Lechón (Liver) Sauce (page 86) or a dip of vinegar, salt and crushed garlic.

Serves 4.

Paksiw Na Lechón • Pork in Liver Sauce

  2 pounds roast pork butt
    (leftover pork roast may be
    used), cut into cubes
  2 cups Lechón Sauce (see page 86)
  1 teaspoon thyme
  1 stick cinnamon
  1 teaspoon oregano
  3 bay leaves
  5 cloves garlic, minced
  1 cup white vinegar
  4 tablespoons soy sauce
salt and freshly ground pepper to taste
  1 tablespoon peppercorns
  4 tablespoons brown sugar

Mix all ingredients in a large enamelware or nonaluminum pot. Boil and simmer for about 2 hours.

Serves 4–6.

Tocino • Cured Pork

2 pounds pork chops or pork loin with fat, sliced into ¼-inch-thick strips
2 tablespoons salt
4 tablespoons sugar
⅛ teaspoon saltpeter (sold in Oriental food stores)

2 tablespoons anise wine or red wine
2 tablespoons anatto water (see page 204)
cooking oil

In a shallow pan, combine all the ingredients except the pork. Sprinkle each piece of pork with the mixture, making sure distribution is even. In a bowl, pile the pork pieces one on top of the other. Cover and keep refrigerated for 3 days to cure.

To cook, put a little water in a skillet and add the pork pieces. Fry the pork until done.

Serves 4.

Humba • Pork Braised with Sugar # 1

1 tablespoon minced garlic
2 tablespoons vegetable or corn oil
1 pound pork shank, cut into 2-inch cubes
1 cup water
2 tablespoons soy sauce
½ cup vinegar

2 tablespoons brown sugar
1 teaspoon salt
½ tablespoon oregano
1 bay leaf
1 heaping tablespoon salted black beans (sold in Oriental food stores)

In a medium pot, sauté garlic in oil until brown. Add pork and cook until brown. Combine water, soy sauce, vinegar, brown sugar, salt, oregano, bay leaf and black beans and add to pork. Cook over low heat until pork is tender. Serve hot.

Serves 3.

Pork Estofado • Pork Braised with Sugar # 2

¼ cup vegetable or corn oil
4 tablespoons minced garlic
1 pound lean pork, cut into cubes
½ cup apple cider vinegar
¼ cup soy sauce
⅓ cup sugar

½ cup water
1 bay leaf
8 peppercorns, crushed
1 carrot, cut into 1-inch strips
2 plantains, cut ½-inch thick diagonally and fried in oil
2 pieces French bread, cut into 1-inch squares and fried in oil

Heat oil and brown garlic. Add pork cubes and fry until brown. Add vinegar, soy sauce, sugar, water, bay leaf and peppercorns. Bring to a boil without stirring. Lower flame and cook until the pork is almost done. Add carrot. Continue cooking until the pork is tender. Before serving, garnish with fried plantains and French bread squares.

Serves 4.

Apritadang Baboy • Pork Stew

5	tablespoons vegetable or corn oil
4	potatoes, peeled and cut into quarters
2	tablespoons minced garlic
2	tablespoons finely chopped onion
2	pounds pork loin, cut into 1½-inch cubes
1	tablespoon salt or to taste
1	cup tomato sauce
2	bay leaves
½	tablespoon freshly ground pepper
½	teaspoon oregano
½	cup pimento-stuffed Spanish olives
½	cup water
6	tablespoons white vinegar
¼	cup bread crumbs
1	red pepper, cored and sliced into ½-inch strips
1	sweet green pepper, cored and sliced into ½-inch strips
1	cup fresh or frozen sweet peas

In a large skillet, heat 2 tablespoons of oil and fry potatoes. Set aside. In a large saucepan, heat 3 tablespoons of oil and sauté garlic and onion until golden brown. Add pork and salt to taste. Cook, stirring often, until pork is tender. Stir in tomato sauce, bay leaves, ground pepper, oregano, olives, water and vinegar. Simmer and keep stirring for 5 minutes. Add bread crumbs, red and green pepper strips and peas. Cook 10 minutes longer.

Serves 4.

Pork Inihaw • Broiled Pork

6   pork chops (or 12 pork spareribs)

Marinade

1   cup white vinegar
2   tablespoons finely minced
    garlic
½   cup sugar
1   tablespoon salt
½   cup soy sauce

Dip

1   cup white vinegar
1   tablespoon finely minced garlic
3   teaspoons red-hot pepper
    sauce

Marinate the pork chops or spareribs overnight. Preheat oven to 425° F for 40 minutes. Broil for 15 minutes, browning both sides (a barbecue grill is preferable). Serve hot with vinegar dip.

Serves 3.

Embutido #1 • Ground Pork Roll

1 ½ pounds ground pork
1 cup bread crumbs, soaked in ½ cup evaporated milk
2 pepperoni sausages, finely chopped
2 eggs, beaten
3 tablespoons sweet pickle relish
3 tablespoons minced seedless raisins
salt and freshly ground pepper to taste
1 small can liver or tomato paste

Mix together all ingredients except the salt and pepper and liver or tomato paste. Roll into a log shape and wrap in aluminum foil. Secure both ends. Bake at 350° F for 1 hour.

Unwrap and transfer the pork roll to a platter. In a small pot, boil the broth in which the pork roll was baked. Thicken with liver or tomato paste and season with salt and pepper. Slice pork roll and pour sauce over it.

Serves 4.

Embutido #2 • Ground Pork Roll

1½ pounds ground pork
1 raw egg
4 tablespoons flour
salt and freshly ground pepper to taste
4 pieces canned Vienna sausage
3 hard-boiled eggs
3 sweet pickles, chopped
catsup

Mix together the ground pork, raw egg, flour, salt and pepper. Spread the mixture on aluminum foil. Arrange the sausages, hard-boiled eggs and pickles on top of the mixture. Shape into a roll about 4 inches in diameter and wrap in foil. Bake for 1 hour at 350° F. Unwrap and slice before serving with catsup.

Serves 4.

Paksiw Na Baboy
• Pork Cooked in Vinegar and Sugar

2 pounds pork butt, cut into 2-inch cubes
2 pounds pigs' knuckles
2 cups white vinegar
½ teaspoon marjoram
4 bay leaves
¼ cup soy sauce
¼ cup brown sugar

salt and freshly ground pepper to taste
5 cloves garlic, minced
3 cups water
1 cup dried banana blossoms (sold in Oriental food stores)
4 ripe plantain bananas, sliced into ½-inch lengths

Combine all ingredients except banana blossoms and plantains in a large saucepan. Bring to a boil and simmer for 2 hours or until pork is tender. Add more water if necessary. (A pressure cooker may be used to reduce cooking time.) Add banana blossoms and plantains and cook for another 15 to 20 minutes. Serve hot.

Serves 4.

Binagoongang Baboy
• Pork Cooked with Shrimp Paste

2	tablespoons vegetable or corn oil
2	tablespoons finely minced garlic
¼	cup chopped onion
¼	cup coarsely chopped tomatoes
1½	pounds boneless pork shoulder or butt, cut into 2-inch cubes
¾	cup water
½	teaspoon sugar
4	tablespoons bagoong or shrimp paste (sold in Oriental food stores)

In a large skillet, heat oil. Sauté the garlic, onion and tomatoes until garlic is brown, onion and tomatoes tender. Add the pork and cook until pork is brown. Add water and simmer for 30 minutes. Add sugar and bagoong or shrimp paste and simmer for 15 minutes until pork is tender, stirring occasionally.

Serves 4.

Menudo • Diced Pork with Potatoes and Chick Peas

2½ cups diced pork
2 cups water
2 tablespoons vegetable or corn oil
2 tablespoons minced garlic
¼ cup chopped onion
½ cup cubed red ripe tomatoes
1 cup diced pork liver
salt to taste
½ cup pimento
2 cups diced potatoes
⅓ cup chick peas, boiled and peeled

In a medium pot, cook the pork in water until tender. Save ½ cup broth. In a medium skillet, heat oil and sauté garlic, onion and tomatoes until garlic is brown, onion is transparent and tomatoes are soft. Add diced pork and liver. Sauté for 5 minutes. Add ½ cup pork broth. Season with salt. Add pimento for color. Add potatoes and chick peas. Simmer for 10 minutes longer. Serve hot.

Serves 4.

Sinigang Na Baboy • Boiled Pork with Lemon

- 2 cloves garlic, crushed
- 1 tablespoon cooking oil
- 1½ cups chopped onion
- 6 medium-size tomatoes, quartered
- 2 slices lemon, squeezed for juice
- 2 pounds pork loin, cut into serving pieces
- 6 cups water
- 3 yams, peeled and quartered
- 1 pound spinach or any green leafy vegetable
- 3 fresh, whole Italian hot green peppers
- 1 tablespoon patis or salt to taste

Sauté garlic in oil until brown. Add onion, tomatoes and lemon juice. Add pork and cook till brown. Add water. Bring to a boil and simmer until pork is tender. When tender, add the yams and simmer until fork-tender. Add the green vegetable, hot peppers, and salt or patis to taste. Cook for another 5 to 7 minutes. Serve hot.

Serves 4.

Almondigas • Pork with Vermicelli

1 egg
1 pound ground pork
1 tablespoon chopped celery
2 tablespoons chopped onion
1 teaspoon garlic powder or 2
   cloves garlic, minced
1 teaspoon salt
⅛ teaspoon pepper
3 cups water
1 bundle vermicelli or misua
   (sold in Oriental food stores)

Beat egg. Add the pork, celery, onion, garlic, salt and pepper. Shape into 1-inch balls. Bring 3 cups of water to a boil and add pork balls. Add vermicelli or misua and simmer for another 5 minutes. Serve hot.

Serves 4.

Sweet-and-Sour Pork

1   pound pork loin, cut into
    serving pieces
3   tablespoons soy sauce
1   teaspoon salt
½   cup cornstarch or flour
oil for frying (enough to cover)
2   cloves garlic, crushed
½   cup chopped onion
1   carrot, cut into small pieces
one 6-ounce can water chestnuts,
    quartered
one 6-ounce can pineapple chunks
    (reserve juice)
½   cup white vinegar
3   tablespoons sugar
1   tablespoon chili oil
1   green pepper, sliced into
    1-inch pieces
1   medium-size tomato,
    quartered

Marinate meat for 3 hours in soy sauce and salt. Dip each piece into cornstarch or flour. Deep fry and set aside. Heat oil and sauté garlic, onion, carrot and water chestnuts. Add juice from pineapple, vinegar, sugar and chili oil. Thicken with 1 tablespoon flour left over from dipping meat.

Add the pork, green pepper and pineapple chunks and cook for 10 minutes. Add the quartered tomato and cook for another 5 minutes. Serve hot.

Serves 4.

Suam Na Baboy
• Boiled Pork with Noodles and Cabbage

    3   cloves garlic, crushed
    3   tablespoons cooking oil
    ¼   cup onion, chopped
    1   small piece of fresh ginger,
          sliced
    ¼   cup patis or 2 tablespoons salt
    2   pounds pork loin, cut into
          cubes
    1   tablespoon peppercorns
    6   cups water
    1   pound cabbage, cut into
          2-by-3-inch slices
    2   bundles vermicelli or misua
          (sold in Oriental food stores)
    1   bunch green onions, diced

Brown garlic in oil and then sauté onion and ginger and season with patis or salt.
Add pork, turning several times to brown. Add peppercorns and water and cook
until pork is tender. Add cabbage and cook for another 5 minutes. Add vermicelli
or misua and green onions and cook for another 5 to 7 minutes. Serve hot.

Serves 8–10.

Crispy Pata • Deep-Fried Pigs' Knuckles

1 pig's knuckle, about 2 pounds
4 cups water
1 tablespoon salt
1 bay leaf
oil for frying (enough to cover)

Dip

½ cup vinegar
3 cloves mashed garlic
salt and pepper to taste

Boil pig's knuckle in water. Add salt and bay leaf. Cook until tender, then deep fry in oil until skin is crispy. Serve with relish or dip of vinegar and garlic.

Serves 2.

Paksiw Na Pata • Pigs' Knuckles

6 pigs' knuckles
4 cups water
1 tablespoon salt
1 cup cooking oil
2 tablespoons finely minced garlic
1 medium-size tomato
¼ cup vinegar
¼ cup soy sauce
1 tablespoon peppercorns
1 bay leaf

In a pressure cooker, boil knuckles in water and salt for about 25 minutes. Or boil 3 hours in regular pot until soft. Drain very well. In a large skillet, heat oil and deep fry the knuckles until golden brown and crisp. Sauté garlic and tomato and add vinegar, soy sauce, peppercorns and bay leaf. Combine mixture with knuckles and boil for 20 minutes. Serve hot.

Serves 4–6.

Hamón • Chinese Ham, Philippine-Style

1 leg cured Chinese ham (about
    3 pounds)
2 cups pineapple juice (approxi-
    mately—see directions, below)
1 6-ounce can pineapple rings

Glaze

4 cups brown sugar
1 cup pineapple juice

Soak ham in water to cover overnight. Then place meat in a large pan and add enough pineapple juice to cover it three-quarters of the way up. Simmer, using 20 minutes per pound as a guide for how long to cook. Trim fat off ham if desired.

Preheat oven to 350° F. Mix brown sugar and pineapple juice and glaze ham with the mixture. Bake for 30 minutes. Cut into serving pieces. Garnish with pineapple rings when serving.

Serves 6–8.

Pata Estofado • Pig's Leg Braised With Sugar

1 large pig's leg, chopped into serving pieces (about 3 pounds)

3 tablespoons oil
5 tablespoons minced garlic
2 large onions, quartered

Marinade

2½ cups apple cider vinegar
1 cup water
10 peppercorns, crushed
½ teaspoon freshly ground black pepper
5 tablespoons brown sugar
¼ cup white wine or gin
½ cup soy sauce
salt to taste
1 teaspoon oregano
1 piece of kamela (cinnamon bark), about ½-inch in size

Garnish

4 plantains, cut ½-inch thick diagonally and fried
2 medium-size yams, cut into thin slices and fried
4 pieces French bread, cut into 1-inch squares and fried

Combine marinade ingredients and marinate pig's leg for 1 hour. Heat oil and brown pig's leg and sauté garlic and onions in a large pot. Pour marinade in, cover the pot and simmer until meat is tender. Transfer meat from the pot to a platter and continue simmering broth until it thickens. Pour broth onto meat and garnish with fried plantains, yams and French-bread squares. Serve hot.

Serves 6–8.

Longaniza • Philippine Sausage

2 pounds ground pork (not too lean—a little fat makes the dish tastier)
1 to 2 tablespoons salt
½ teaspoon freshly ground pepper
½ cup white vinegar

2 tablespoons minced garlic
2 teaspoons paprika
¼ teaspoon saltpeter (can be bought in Oriental food stores)
1 teaspoon brown sugar
2 yards pork casings (sold in Italian meat stores)

Season pork with salt. Add pepper, vinegar, garlic, paprika, saltpeter and sugar. Mix well and let stand for 1 to 2 hours. Stuff the mixture into the casings. Tie at both ends. Keep in the refrigerator in a tightly covered container for 24 hours. Then cook on top of stove over low heat in a little water until the water evaporates and pork fat appears. Fry in its own fat and serve hot.

Serves 4–6.

Pata Rellenada • Stuffed Pig's Leg

1   whole pig's leg, boned and
     meat removed as well, leaving
     both the skin and the end hoof
     intact (a butcher will do this if
     requested)

Stuffing

½   cup chopped cooked ham
2   teaspoons minced parsley
salt and freshly ground pepper to
       taste
1   large egg
2   tablespoons white wine
needle and thread

Stew

2   cups water
½   cup soy sauce
10   whole peppercorns, crushed
1   tablespoon sugar
½   cup white wine
1   tablespoon cornstarch

Relish (Achara) (see page 198)

Chop the meat. Combine with ham, parsley, salt and pepper. Add egg and wine.

Fill the skin and hoof case with the mixture. Sew the thigh end securely with strong thread. Put the stuffed *pata* in a medium-size stockpot with the stewing ingredients and cook over low heat until skin is tender. Remove from pot, cool and slice thin.

Use the leftover gravy from the pot as sauce and thicken with 1 tablespoon cornstarch.

Serve with relish.

Serves 6–8.

Bachoy • Sautéed Pork with Kidney and Liver

½ pound pork loin, cubed
⅓ pound beef kidney, cubed
⅓ pound beef liver, cubed
⅓ pound beef pancreas, cubed
1 cup vegetable or corn oil
1 tablespoon finely minced garlic
¼ cup finely minced onion
2 tablespoons finely minced
  ginger
3 cups water
1 tablespoon patis or salt
½ teaspoon freshly ground
  pepper
½ pound spinach

Clean the meats thoroughly. In a medium skillet, heat 1 tablespoon oil and fry all the meat cubes until brown. Drain and set aside.

In another medium skillet, heat 2 tablespoons oil and sauté garlic, onion and ginger. Cook until garlic is brown and onion is transparent. Add the fried meat cubes. Add water and bring to a boil. Simmer until the meats are tender. Season with patis or salt and pepper. Add spinach and cook until wilted. Serve hot.

Serves 4.

Tamales

3½ cups rice
6 cups coconut milk
1 cup brown sugar
salt and freshly ground pepper to
    taste
1 cup ground roast peanuts
½ cup anatto water (see
    page 204)
12 banana leaves (available in
    Hispanic food stores), or 12
    pieces aluminum foil cut into
    10-by-12-inch pieces
2 chicken breasts, boiled and
    sliced in ½-inch pieces
1 pound pork butt, boiled and
    sliced in ½-inch pieces
1 pound shrimps, shelled,
    deveined and boiled
1 pound cooked ham, sliced in
    ½-inch pieces
2 hard-boiled eggs, sliced
2 cups peanuts, boiled until soft

In a food processor, grind rice until powdery. In a deep saucepan, combine coconut milk, powdered rice, sugar, salt and pepper and cook over low heat for 25 minutes, stirring occasionally to prevent sticking. Add ground roast peanuts and cook for 6 minutes, stirring occasionally. Remove half the mixture from the saucepan and set aside. This will be the regular mixture. To the remaining sauce in the pan, add the anatto water and continue cooking for 5 minutes, stirring occasionally. This will be the red mixture.

On a banana leaf or piece of foil, place 3 tablespoonfuls of the regular mixture and shape into a 3-inch square. Arrange slices of chicken, pork, shrimps, ham, eggs and boiled peanuts on top of the square. Cover with 3 tablespoons of red mixture. This will create a layered look when the squares are opened. Wrap the mixture in the leaf or piece of foil. Repeat the process until all the mixture is gone. Arrange the wrapped squares on a steamer and steam for 20 minutes.

Serves 6–8.

7

Beef Dishes

Most of the recipes in this section are of Spanish origin. This is because beef was virtually unknown in Philippine cuisine until the Spanish introduced it. The first beef cattle brought to the Philippines made the long, arduous trek across the Pacific from Mexico in leaky, unsanitary Spanish ships. Only the strongest animals survived—and for many years this was reflected in the quality of the beef available. After the American occupation of the islands, around the turn of the century, cattle raising took on more importance, as the Americans found it difficult to get by without their regular rations of beef.

The Batangas area, south of Manila, and the island of Mindanao, are the two prime areas for cattle raising. The animals are grass fed, which makes the beef tough—long, slow cooking and marinating are therefore used to make the local beef achieve the necessary tenderness. Some grain-fed beef is imported from Australia and New Zealand.

Beef dishes are growing in popularity in the Philippines, and bistek is a favorite. However, pork, fish and chicken will probably remain supreme as the principle sources of protein for most Filipinos.

Empanada • Meat Turnover

1 pound ground beef
1 clove garlic, minced, or ½
  teaspoon garlic powder
1 small onion, minced
1 cup diced potatoes
1 teaspoon salt
¼ teaspoon pepper
½ cup seedless raisins

Brown ground beef. Push meat to one side and sauté garlic until brown, then add onion. Mix the meat, garlic and onion, then add potatoes. Stir and cook until potatoes are tender. Season with salt and pepper and mix in raisins.

Pastry (Ready-made pie-crust mix may also be used)

3 cups all-purpose flour
4 tablespoons sugar
½ teaspoon salt
½ cup water
⅓ cup oil
3 egg yolks (plus some egg
  whites for sealing empanadas)

Mix and knead all ingredients until dough is soft. On a floured board, roll out ⅛ inch thick. Cut into 4- or 5-inch-diameter circles (use wide-mouthed jar or cup for cutting circles). Put a spoonful of meat filling in center of each circle. Fold to half-moon shape, wet edges with egg white, press and seal sides. Deep fry until golden brown and drain. Or, instead of deep frying, pies can be baked in preheated 425° F oven for 15 to 20 minutes or until golden brown.

Yield: 20 empanadas

Mechado • Beef Stew with a Wick

Mecha is the Spanish word for "wick," the fiber core of a candle. Beef in the Philippines is usually very lean, as cows are grass-fed. In order to give the dish more taste, fat or bacon is inserted in the meat.

2   to 3 pounds lean beef (rolled
      roast, chuck steak or
      London broil)
juice of one lemon
4 to 5 tablespoons soy sauce
2   strips bacon
1   bay leaf
8-ounce can tomato sauce
3   tablespoons sherry
3   cloves crushed garlic
salt to taste
2   cups water
2 to 3 tablespoons flour
2   tablespoons butter
1   teaspoon chopped pimento
4   big onions, quartered
6   potatoes, quartered

Marinate beef in lemon juice and soy sauce. Make 2 lengthwise slits in the meat and insert the bacon strips. In a large pot, brown the meat, then add the bay leaf, tomato sauce, the marinade, sherry, garlic, salt and water. Cover the pot and simmer until the beef is tender. Remove meat and slice. Thicken sauce with flour and butter. Add pimento, onions and potatoes with the meat to the thickened sauce. Serve hot.

Serves 4–6.

Morcón • Meat Roll

　2　pounds beef flank
　2　tablespoons lemon juice
　¼　cup soy sauce
pepper to taste
　1　can Vienna sausage
　6　pieces sweet pickles
　4　strips bacon
　2　slices sharp cheddar cheese
　½　cup stuffed olives
　2　hard-boiled eggs, halved
　　　lengthwise
　1　carrot, quartered lengthwise
　4　tablespoons cooking oil
　1　garlic clove, crushed
　1　small onion, chopped
　1　cup tomato sauce
　3　cups water
salt and freshly ground pepper to
　　　taste
parsley for garnish

Marinate beef in lemon juice, soy sauce and pepper to taste for 10 minutes. Drain and save marinade. Spread beef flank and arrange on it, in lengthwise rows, Vienna sausage, sweet pickles, bacon, cheese, olives, hard-boiled eggs and carrot. Roll with meat grain lengthwise and tie with a string. Simmer in oil in a mixture of marinade, garlic, onion, tomato sauce and water for 1 hour or until meat is tender. Season with salt and pepper to taste.

Transfer meat roll to a platter, remove string and slice crosswise into ½-inch thicknesses. Pour sauce over meat and garnish with parsley.

Serves 6–8.

Bistek • Steak, Philippine-Style*

2 pounds sirloin steak, cut into
¼-inch pieces

2 tablespoons lemon juice

3 tablespoons soy sauce

½ teaspoon freshly ground
pepper

salt to taste

1 cup thinly sliced onion rings

¼ cup cooking oil

½ cup water

Marinate the meat in lemon juice, soy sauce, pepper and salt for 3 hours or more. Cook onion rings in oil until transparent. Transfer to a serving dish, leaving the oil in the skillet. Add the meat to the skillet and cook over high heat, stirring often, until tender. Transfer the meat to a serving dish. Add marinade and water to the skillet, simmer for 10 minutes and pour over the meat and onion rings.

Serves 4.

Karne Asada • Beef Stew

2 pounds beef sirloin, cut into
3-inch cubes

2 tablespoons lemon juice

2 tablespoons soy sauce

1½ tablespoons cornstarch

¼ teaspoon Maggi sauce
(available in Oriental stores) or

soy sauce

patis or salt and freshly ground
pepper to taste

2 large potatoes, sliced in rounds

2 large onions, sliced in rings

3 tablespoons oil

Marinate the sirloin cubes in lemon juice, soy sauce, cornstarch, Maggi, patis or salt and pepper for 30 minutes. Then, over a low flame, simmer the marinade and the sirloin for 1 hour. In a skillet, fry potatoes and onion rings in oil separately. Arrange beef on a platter with potatoes and onion rings on top.

Serves 4.

*This recipe can also be used for pork chops, liver or fish.

Tortilla • Ground Beef Omelet

1 tablespoon cooking oil	¼ teaspoon pepper
1 tablespoon finely minced garlic	1 cup diced potatoes
½ cup diced onion	1 teaspoon finely minced parsley
¼ cup diced tomatoes	1 cup water
1 pound ground beef	3 well-beaten eggs
1½ teaspoons salt	

In a large skillet, heat oil and sauté garlic, onion and tomatoes. Garlic is done when brown and onion when transparent. Stir in ground beef and cook for 5 minutes or until brown. Pour off excess fat. Season with salt and pepper. Add potatoes, parsley and water. Cover and cook 15 minutes more or until potatoes are tender and most of the water has evaporated. Cool.

Add beaten eggs to meat mixture. Heat just enough oil to cover the bottom of a medium skillet. Pour in the mixture and cook over medium heat for 2 to 5 minutes on one side. Flip the omelet and cook on other side for 2 to 3 minutes. Serve with tomato catsup.

Serves 2–4.

Picadillo • Ground Beef Soup

  3   tablespoons minced garlic
  1   tablespoon oil
  ½ cup minced shallots
  1   cup cubed tomatoes
  ½ pound ground beef (preferably
      round)
  ½ pound ground pork
patis or salt and freshly ground
      pepper to taste
  4   cups water
  2   cups diced potatoes

In a saucepan, sauté garlic in oil until brown. Add shallots and tomatoes and cook till soft. Add ground beef, pork, patis or salt and pepper to taste. Add water and potatoes. Simmer until done. Serve hot.

Sinigang Na Karne • Boiled Beef

 2 pounds stewing beef or beef
    shank, cut into 1-inch cubes
 2 pounds spare ribs (separate
    each rib)
½ cup minced onion
 4 cups cubed red ripe tomatoes
 2 cups rhubarb, cut crosswise
    into 2-inch slices (if rhubarb is
    not available, substitute 6
    tablespoons lime or lemon
    juice)
 6 cups water
patis or salt and freshly ground
    pepper to taste
 2 cups spinach or any green
    leafy vegetable
1½ cups red radish
 2 cups green cabbage, quartered

To a large stockpot, add the beef, spare ribs, onion, tomatoes and rhubarb in 6 cups water. Bring to a boil; skim off foam; then simmer until tender. Remove rhubarb and mash. Strain through a sieve and return extract to pot. Add patis or salt and pepper to taste. Put in the leafy vegetable, radish and cabbage. Simmer until vegetables are done.

Serves 6–8.

Lomo Guisado • Sautéed Beef Strips

 3 tablespoons cooking oil
 2 tablespoons minced garlic
 ½ cup minced onion
 1 tablespoon fresh ginger cut
    into ⅛-inch slices.
 3 fresh tomatoes, cut up but
    with skin and seeds remaining
 2 pounds beef tenderloin or
    round steak, cut into 2-inch
    strips
 ¼ cup soy sauce
 5 cups beef broth or beef
    bouillon
salt and pepper to taste

Heat oil in a small skillet. Sauté garlic until brown. Add onion, ginger and tomatoes. Add beef strips, then soy sauce. Add beef broth or bouillon ½ cup at a time and simmer until meat is tender. Make sure there is enough broth to cover the beef strips. Season with salt and pepper. Serve hot.

Serves 4–6.

Karne con Kutsay • Beef with Leeks

1	pound beef tenderloin, cut in 1½-inch cubes
1	egg white
1	tablespoon cornstarch
1	cup cooking oil
3	tablespoons soy sauce
3	tablespoons water
1	red pepper, cut into strips
¼	cup kutsay or leeks cut into strips
2	tablespoons sesame oil

Coat tenderloin with egg white, then with cornstarch. Let stand for 15 minutes. Deep fry in oil and drain. Leave 3 tablespoons of oil in pan. Add soy sauce, water, red pepper, leeks and meat. Cook for 2 minutes. Add sesame oil before serving.

Serves 4.

Pocherong Baka • Beef Pochero-Style

1 to 2 pounds sirloin steak, cut into small pieces
6 cups water
1 potato, quartered
1 ripe plantain, cut into serving pieces
2 cloves garlic, crushed
2 tablespoons oil
1 chorizo de Bilbao or pepperoni

6-ounce can chick peas
¼ pound green beans
½ medium-size green cabbage, sliced
1 bunch green onions or scallions
1 small onion, quartered
8 peppercorns
salt to taste

Simmer beef in water until tender. Set aside broth. Boil potato in beef broth and set aside. Boil plantain and set aside. In a large skillet or saucepan, brown garlic in oil. Add beef, chorizo or pepperoni, chick peas, broth, green beans, cabbage and green onions or scallions. Also add quartered onion and peppercorns. Simmer until vegetables are done. Add salt to taste. When ready to serve, garnish with banana and potato. Serve with pochero sauce.

Pochero Sauce

1 medium-size eggplant
½ plantain, peeled and boiled
1 small sweet potato or yam, peeled and boiled

¼ cup white vinegar
1 clove garlic, finely crushed
salt and pepper to taste

Boil eggplant and remove skin and mash with plantain and sweet potato. Add the vinegar, garlic, salt and pepper and heat.

Serves 5–6.

Higadillo • Sautéed Liver

2 tablespoons finely minced garlic
1 cup minced onion
3 tablespoons vegetable or corn oil
2 cups cubed ripe tomatoes
1 pound pork loin, sliced thin in ½-inch squares
1 pound liver (pork or beef)
½ cup white vinegar
¼ cup sugar
patis or salt and freshly ground pepper

Sauté garlic and onion in hot oil till onion is transparent. Stir in tomatoes and cook until soft. Add pork and liver and cook till tender. Stir in vinegar and sugar and simmer over low heat. Season with patis or salt and pepper to taste.

Serves 6.

Kare-Kare • Oxtail Stew in Peanut-Butter Sauce

3	pounds oxtail, cut into serving pieces
8	cups water
2	tablespoons finely minced garlic
1	cup chopped onion
4	tablespoons cooking oil
½	cup anatto water (see page 204)
½	cup raw rice, ground to a powder in a food processor and roasted in a pan
1	cup peanut butter
1	eggplant, cut into serving pieces
10	string beans, cut into 2-inch lengths
1	small cabbage, quartered

salt and freshly ground pepper to taste

Boil oxtail in 8 cups water for 2 hours or until tender. Set stock aside. Sauté garlic and onion in oil in a large saucepan. Discard anatto seeds and add anatto water and oxtail to saucepan and bring to a boil. Stir in roast rice powder and peanut butter. Add four cups reserved stock, eggplant, string beans and cabbage and mix well. Bring to a boil and simmer for 10 minutes. Season with salt and pepper to taste. Serve with bagoong or shrimp paste.

Serves 6–8.

Lengua con Setas • Ox Tongue with Chick Peas

    4   pounds ox tongue, cleaned
    5   tablespoons cooking oil
    3   teaspoons salt
    2   teaspoons freshly ground
        pepper
   ½   cup white wine
    2   tablespoons cooking oil
    1   cup chopped onion
   ½   cup tomato sauce
    2   cups canned cooked chick peas
    1   cup water
   ¼   cup bread crumbs

Boil tongue in water to cover until tender. Drain. Fry in oil until brown. Slice tongue and marinate 1 hour in salt, pepper and white wine. Set aside. In a medium skillet, heat oil. Sauté onion and sliced tongue. Add tomato sauce, chick peas and marinade and 1 cup of water. Simmer for 15 minutes or until sauce is thick and tongue is tender. Add bread crumbs to thicken sauce. Serve hot.

Serves 6.

Lengua con Champignon
• Ox Tongue with Mushroom

1　ox tongue
1　tablespoon lemon juice
¼　cup soy sauce
¼　cup olive oil
½　cup butter
5　cloves garlic, minced
2　medium onions, chopped
⅓　cup fresh chopped tomatoes
3　tablespoons peppercorns
¼　cup white wine

Boil ox tongue in large pot of water for 15 minutes. Drain. Peel off or scrape outer skin. Trim root ends and wash thoroughly. Marinate tongue in lemon juice and soy sauce for 1 hour. Brown in olive oil and butter. Set aside.

In the same pan, sauté garlic, onions and tomatoes. Put back tongue and add peppercorns and white wine. Bring to a boil, then simmer for 3 hours or until tongue is tender. (A pressure cooker may be used to lessen cooking time.) Slice tongue and arrange on a platter. Set aside sauce. Serve with mushroom-butter sauce.

Mushroom-Butter Sauce

½　cup butter
¼　cup all-purpose flour
½　cup sliced mushrooms
sauce from tongue

Melt butter in skillet. Blend in flour. Add the mushrooms and sauce. Bring to a boil. Water may be added if sauce is too thick. Pour over sliced meat and serve.

Serves 6.

Lengua Estofado • Beef Tongue Braised with Sugar

4 to 5 pounds beef tongue

Marinade

1 cup water
1 teaspoon whole peppercorns
1 bay leaf
3 tablespoons apple cider
   vinegar or white cooking wine
3 tablespoons soy sauce
3 tablespoons sugar
2 teaspoons salt

3 tablespoons cooking oil
5 tablespoons minced garlic
½ cup minced onion
½ cup minced tomatoes
2 potatoes, quartered
2 cups carrots, cut into strips
salt and pepper to taste
⅓ cup stuffed olives
⅓ cup mushrooms, cut in half

Boil tongue in a large pot of water for 15 minutes. Drain. Peel off or scrape the outer skin. Trim the root ends and wash thoroughly. Mix all marinade ingredients and marinate the beef tongue for 40 minutes. In a large pot, heat oil and brown the tongue. Remove tongue but leave oil. In remaining oil, sauté garlic till brown, then onion and tomatoes until soft. Put tongue back in the pot. Pour in marinade and simmer for 2½ hours or until the tongue is tender. Add water as needed and prick tongue to let liquid penetrate. (A pressure cooker may be used to lessen cooking time.) Remove tongue and slice. Return slices to pot, add potatoes and carrots and simmer until vegetables are tender. Season with salt and pepper. Add stuffed olives and mushrooms. Serve hot.

Serves 8 or more.

Pastel de Lengua • Ox Tongue Pie

5 pounds calf or ox tongue	cut crosswise into
5 cups water	⅛-inch-thick slices
2 tablespoons whole	5 tablespoons sherry
peppercorns	5 tablespoons parmesan cheese
2 onions, quartered	1 cup carrots cut into ½-inch
3 bay leaves	cubes
4 ounces butter	2 tablespoons flour, dissolved in
½ cup finely minced onion	3 tablespoons water
1 cup minced fresh mushrooms	5 medium-size potatoes, peeled
2 chorizos de Bilbao or	and cut into small cubes
pepperoni cut crosswise into	½ cup pimento-stuffed olives
⅛-inch-thick slices	salt and pepper to taste
1 cup canned Vienna sausage,	1 egg, beaten

Boil tongue in 5 cups water, with peppercorns, quartered onions and bay leaves till tender. Let cool and set aside. Reserve 2 cups broth.

Sauté butter, minced onion and mushrooms. Add chorizos de Bilbao or pepperoni, Vienna sausage and boiled tongue. Cook till sausages become tender. Add reserved broth and continue boiling. Stir in sherry, parmesan cheese, carrots and potatoes. Cook till vegetables are done. Add flour-water mixture, olives, salt and pepper.

Preheat oven to 350° F. Transfer filling to a baking dish. Cover with pie crust. Seal the edges of the crust around the dish by fluting. Brush top of crust with beaten egg and bake for 10 minutes.

Pie Crust

1½ cups all-purpose flour
4 ounces butter
½ teaspoon cold water

Mix flour and butter until well blended. Add water gradually and roll out dough. Use to cover the pastel.

Serves 6.

Callos Madrileña
• Tripe with Chick Peas

2 pounds tripe
6 cups water with 3 tablespoons salt
8 strips bacon
2 cups potatoes cut into ½-inch-thick slices
3 chorizos de Bilbao or pepperoni, sliced in ⅛-inch rounds

1 cup cooked canned chick peas
2 8-ounce cans tomato sauce
salt and freshly ground pepper to taste
2 cups water
2 tablespoons diced pimento
1 cup tomato catsup

Boil the tripe in 6 cups salted water until tender (a pressure cooker may be used for faster cooking). Discard all fat. Rinse the tripe and cut into ½-inch squares. Set aside.

In a large skillet, fry the bacon. Remove and set aside. In the same skillet, fry potatoes, chorizos or pepperoni and chick peas. Add tomato sauce. Season with salt and pepper. Add bacon and tripe and 2 cups of water. Stir. Cover and simmer over low heat for 20 minutes. Add pimento and tomato catsup; add a little water if the mixture is too dry. Stir to blend flavors and serve hot.

Serves 4–6.

Kalderetta • Goat Stew*

3 to 4 pounds goat meat, cut into
    2-inch pieces
¾ cup white vinegar
1 head garlic, crushed
salt and freshly ground pepper to
    taste
¼ cup cooking oil
½ cup sliced onion
¼ cup sherry
½ cup olive oil
1 small bay leaf
1 sprig parsley, chopped
1 teaspoon white peppercorns,
    crushed

6 cloves garlic, crushed
1 hot green pepper
½ cup tomato sauce
2 cups warm water
1 slice goat liver (about 5 inches
    square and ½ inch thick)
½ cup water
1 cup pimento
½ cup grated cheddar cheese
1 teaspoon sugar
dash of hot sauce
1 cup green olives

Marinate meat in a mixture of vinegar, garlic, salt and pepper for 24 hours. Drain meat and brown several pieces at a time in hot oil. Place meat, onion and sherry in a saucepan. Bring to a boil, then add olive oil and bay leaf. Add parsley, peppercorns, garlic and hot pepper. Then add tomato sauce and water. Simmer until meat is tender.

    Brown the goat liver and then pound to a paste. Add ½ cup water to liver and add to the meat, stirring occasionally, until mixture comes to a boil. Add the pimento and the grated cheese. Season with sugar and hot sauce to taste, then add the olives. Serve hot.

Serves 8.

---

*Lamb or beef may also be used for this recipe.

8

Fish and Shellfish Dishes

The Filipinos are fish-eating people. Innumerable varieties of fish and shellfish can be found in the rivers, lakes and surrounding ocean without great effort. *Palaisdaan* (fish ponds) abound in estuaries and alongside riverbanks, and deep-sea fishing constitutes the principal industry of many regions.

The most popular fish cultivated in ponds is the *bangus,* or milkfish. Many people would consider this a bony fish, but its delicious flavor and adaptability to various recipes make the job of picking bones well worth the effort. *Bangus* is exported from the Philippines and available frozen in Filipino grocery stores and some Oriental stores, too. Smoked *bangus* and some other varieties of fish are also available in the United States in these stores.

The most popular ocean fishes are *lapu-lapu* (grouper) and *apahap* (snapper). These fish can be found with fair regularity at most United States fish markets. Mullet, a fish not very popular in the United States, is served roasted or broiled in the Philippines. *Banak,* as it is known there, is excellent.

The variety of lobsters and crabs that can be seen at Manila fish markets is astounding. About 8 species of lobsters and 16 species of crabs are commonly eaten. Giant river prawns and shrimps of many sizes, unlike the varieties available in the United States, are common at the Manila markets.

For most of the recipes in this section, any readily available fish can be used in lieu of the fish that would be used in the Philippines, with no detriment to the dish.

Lobsters

There are six kinds of lobsters that are commonly eaten in the Philippines. All are of the spiny variety, similar to the ones found in tropical waters around the globe. These lobsters do not have the massive claws that lobsters taken from cold waters have, or the same flavor. The meat in the tail, where the legs join the body and around the head is delicious.

Lobster is considered such a treat in the Philippines that it is rarely served other than simply steamed. A sauce of white vinegar and crushed garlic is often served with it for dipping.

Pesang Dalag • Fish Stew

1 pound grouper, filleted
2 teaspoons salt
2 teaspoons cooking oil
1 piece fresh ginger root, peeled and sliced into julienne strips
1 small onion, quartered
3 cups water
10 peppercorns, crushed
½ cup leeks or scallions, sliced
1 cabbage, quartered
1 bunch Chinese lettuce, cut into 3-inch pieces
patis or salt to taste
freshly ground pepper to taste

Season the fish fillets with salt. In a medium saucepan, heat oil and sauté ginger and onion. When onion turns transparent, add water and peppercorns. Bring to a boil. Add the fish. Bring to a quick second boil. Turn off heat. Add leeks or scallions, cabbage and Chinese lettuce. Season with patis or salt and pepper to taste. Serve hot with misu-tomato sauce.

Misu-Tomato Sauce

1 teaspoon cooking oil
1 teaspoon finely minced garlic
½ cup chopped onion
½ cup finely minced ripe tomatoes
2 tablespoons salted bean paste (misu)
½ teaspoon apple cider vinegar
½ teaspoon freshly ground pepper

In a small skillet, heat oil and sauté garlic until light brown, then onion until transparent and tomatoes until soft. Add bean paste. Mix and mash the whole mixture with a fork. Add vinegar and pepper. Bring to a boil. Serve with boiled fish.

Serves 4.

Lapu-Lapu Relleno • Stuffed Sea Bass

  2 pounds lapu-lapu or any white
    fish, preferably sea bass (red
    snapper may also be
    substituted)
  2 hard-boiled eggs, sliced
  2 cups diced cooked ham
  ¼ cup flour
  ½ cup olive oil
  1 tablespoon minced garlic
  1 tablespoon lemon juice
  1 cup stuffed green olives
sprig of parsley as garnish

Clean fish. Slit open at back and bone. Stuff with alternating layers of egg and ham. Tie securely with a string. Dredge in flour. Set aside in a baking pan.

Preheat oven to 350° F. Heat the olive oil and sauté the garlic until brown. Pour over the fish. Bake the fish for about 7 minutes until half done, basting with pan oil occasionally. Remove the pan from the oven and pour lemon juice and Spanish tomato sauce (see recipe, page 202) over it. Return to oven and bake 15 minutes more. Arrange on a platter and garnish with olives and parsley. Serve hot.

Serves 4–6.

Kardillong Isda • Sautéed Fish with Egg

1½ teaspoons salt
1½ tablespoons lemon juice
one 2-pound fish, whole or sliced
　　　into quarters, or any
　　　1½-pound fish fillet
½ cup flour (optional)
1 cup cooking oil
2 cloves garlic, crushed
¼ cup sliced onion
¾ cup diced ripe tomato
½ cup water
salt and pepper to taste
2 eggs, slightly beaten

Sprinkle salt and lemon juice on fish. Fry in oil until brown. (When using fish fillets, shake each fillet in a small plastic bag with ½ cup flour before frying.) Use 2 tablespoons of oil for frying if fish is not floured; 3 tablespoons if it is. Set aside. In 3 tablespoons hot oil sauté garlic until brown; add onion and tomato. Cook until onion is transparent and tomato is soft. Add fried fish and water. Simmer for 5 minutes. Season with salt and pepper. Add slightly beaten eggs. Simmer for another 2 minutes. Serve hot.

Serves 4–6.

Pescado al Horno • Baked Fish

6 to 8 fillets of lapu-lapu (red snapper or grouper may be substituted)
1 teaspoon lemon juice
salt and freshly ground pepper to taste
⅓ cup olive oil

1 whole onion, finely minced
1½ cups fresh chopped tomatoes, with skin and seeds
½ cup pimento cut into strips
1 tablespoon finely minced parsley
1 tablespoon bread crumbs

Preheat oven to 350° F. Season the fillets with lemon juice, salt and pepper and place in a shallow glass pan. Set aside. In a medium skillet, heat olive oil. Sauté onions, tomatoes and pimento until a saucelike consistency is obtained. Pour the sauce on the fish. Sprinkle the fish with parsley and bread crumbs. Bake at 350° F for 25 minutes. Serve hot.

Serves 4.

Fish Tinola • Boiled Fish

1 tablespoon vegetable or corn oil	2 cups water
1 cup chopped onion	1 pound whole fish
1 tablespoon finely minced garlic	2 cups sliced zucchini
1 tablespoon finely minced ginger	patis or salt to taste
	½ teaspoon freshly ground pepper

In a medium saucepan, heat oil. Sauté onion, garlic and ginger. Add water and bring to a boil. Add fish and zucchini. Season with patis or salt and pepper and simmer until done. Serve hot.

Serves 2.

Mullet is a species of fish that is largely ignored in the United States yet commonly sought after in Asia. In the Philippines, mullet are an incidental element in fish ponds, but there are plans to raise them with milkfish, carp and other species in a common pond. This method of raising numerous species in one pond is known as polyculture. It takes advantage of the fact that different species have different feeding habits and can survive and thrive without competing for food. In many cases, the presence of other species is mutually beneficial.

In the Philippines, tilapia is one of the most popular fish. Though tilapia has been a source of food throughout recorded history, and even thought to be the fish Christ fed to the multitudes, it is not available in supermarkets in the United States.

In the United States, the common carp found in the wild is not a very popular fish. This is because it is generally scaly, bony and coarse textured. Pond-raised varieties are quite different and very delicious. In Asia, carp is one of the most popular fish and has been for three thousand years.

Pescado con Salsa Blanca • Fish with White Sauce

  1   2-pound sea bass
  1   tablespoon lemon juice
salt and pepper to taste
  2   onions, minced
  ¼   cup cubed red ripe tomatoes
  3   tablespoons white wine
  2   cups celery, sliced into 1-inch
       pieces
1½   cups water
  ⅛   cup butter (4 tablespoons or ½
       stick)
  2   tablespoons flour
  ⅓   cup milk
salt and pepper to taste

Preheat oven to 350° F. Clean fish thoroughly. Rub with lemon juice inside and out. Season fish with salt and pepper and put in a baking dish.

Add onion, tomatoes, white wine, celery and water. Bake at 350° F for 45 minutes. Strain the sauce, and keep fish warm.

In a large skillet, melt the butter. Remove from the fire. Add flour and strained fish sauce and simmer over low heat until sauce becomes thick. Add milk. Simmer for 2 minutes. Season with salt and pepper to taste. Pour the sauce on the fish. Serve hot.

Serves 4−6.

Fish Sarciado • Fish with Tomato Sauce

1 pound fish fillets (sole, red
   snapper or sea bass)
1 teaspoon salt
1 tablespoon lemon juice
½ cup vegetable or corn oil
2 tablespoons minced garlic
¼ cup minced onion
1 cup minced tomatoes
½ teaspoon freshly ground
   pepper
¼ cup water
1 teaspoon patis or salt
¼ cup chopped scallions

Season the fish with salt and lemon juice. Let stand for 20 minutes.

In a large skillet, using half the oil, fry the fillets until they are light brown on both sides. Drain on absorbent paper towel. In another large skillet, sauté garlic in remaining oil until light brown, then onion until transparent and tomatoes until soft. Add pepper, water and patis or salt. Simmer until a saucy consistency is achieved. Add the fried fish to the sauce. Cover the skillet and cook for 2 minutes, turning the fillets once. Serve hot, garnished with scallions.

Serves 4.

Rellenong Bangus • Stuffed Milkfish

3 pounds bangus, dressed (weak fish, tilefish or sea bass may be substituted)
salt and freshly ground pepper to taste
1 cup cooking oil
1 tablespoon minced garlic
1 cup minced onion
1½ cups cubed ripe tomatoes
1 tablespoon lemon juice
½ cup cooked peas
¼ cup minced seedless raisins
1 egg, slightly beaten

Clean the fish. Cut open at back. Remove the meat of the fish. Free of all spines. Set aside the spineless fish skin. Flake the fish. Season with salt and pepper.

Heat oil in pan and sauté garlic until brown, then onion until transparent and ½ cup tomatoes until soft. Add flaked fish and cook well. Add lemon juice, peas, raisins and remaining tomatoes and cook for another minute or two.

Remove from fire. Add slightly beaten egg. Fill bangus with mixture and sew up the opening. Deep fry until fish is golden brown, turning once.

Serves 6–8.

Paksiw Na Bangus • Milkfish Stew

1 pound milkfish (can be bought in Filipino stores, or whitefish, mullet, butterfish or porgy may be substituted)

1 cup quartered bitter melon (optional)

½ cup ginger sliced ½-inch lengthwise and pounded

1 cup quartered eggplant

3 hot green peppers

1 cup white vinegar

¾ cup water

patis or salt to taste

Clean bangus and cut into three serving pieces. Arrange bitter melon, ginger and eggplant in nonaluminum saucepan and place fish and whole peppers over vegetables. Add vinegar and bring to a boil. Add water and continue simmering until fish is cooked. Add patis or salt to taste. Paksiw is better served aged. Store in refrigerator in a covered dish for one to two days. Reheat when ready to serve.

Serves 2–4.

Inihaw Na Bangus • Broiled Milkfish

2 pounds milkfish (whitefish or sea bass may be substituted)

2 lemon slices

1½ teaspoons salt

⅛ teaspoon freshly ground black pepper

½ cup finely minced tomatoes

½ cup finely minced onion

2 stalks finely minced scallions

1 tablespoon lemon juice

4 tablespoons soy sauce

With a very sharp knife, cut the fish along its back and remove the backbone. Rub fish inside and out with lemon. Season with salt and pepper.

In a bowl, mix tomatoes, onion and scallions. Stuff the fish with the mixture. Secure the end. Wrap in foil loosely and broil for 10 minutes or until fish is cooked. Serve with a dip of lemon juice and soy sauce mixed together.

Serves 4.

Sopa de Mariscos • Fish Soup

This is similar to the French bouillabaisse.

2 pounds fillets of any fish with white meat
3 cups water
1 cup chopped leeks
1 onion, quartered
30 clams
½ cup minced onion
1 cup tomato sauce
¼ cup olive oil
salt and freshly ground pepper to taste
1 teaspoon sugar
2 tablespoons minced garlic
¼ cup croutons
2 tablespoons raw rice
½ pound squid, sliced into ½-inch-thick rings
½ pound medium-size shrimps, shelled and deveined
2 cups fresh or frozen crabmeat, cooked
salt and freshly ground pepper to taste
2 hard-boiled eggs, sliced
2 tablespoons minced parsley

In a small pot, boil fish fillets in water with the onion and leeks. Strain and set aside the stock. Cut fish into chunks. Set aside.

In a small pot, boil clams in enough water to cover until they open. Strain and set aside clam stock. Remove clams from their shells.

In a small skillet, sauté onion and tomato sauce in 1 tablespoon of olive oil. Season with salt, pepper and sugar. Set aside.

In a large saucepan, heat the rest of the olive oil and brown the garlic. Remove garlic and set aside. Fry the croutons in the same oil. Remove and set aside. Add the rice, squid and shrimps. Pour in all of the fish stock and simmer for 20 minutes. Add clam broth if more liquid is desired. Add the fish, clams, crabmeat and tomato sauce and garlic bits. Mix everything well, adding more clam broth as needed. Season with salt and pepper. Add croutons.

Transfer to a serving dish. Serve hot, garnished with egg slices and parsley.

Serves 6–8.

Pastel de Pescado • Fish Pie

Pastry

  2   cups flour
  1   teaspoon salt
  ½ cup cooking oil
  ¼ cup cold water

Combine flour and salt in a bowl. Make a well in the center and add oil and cold water. Stir and mix lightly into a ball. Set aside. (You can also use a pie-crust mix.)

Filling

  2   pounds grouper or sea bass, boned and cut into chunks
  1   tablespoon lemon juice
  1   teaspoon salt
  ¼ teaspoon freshly ground pepper
  ⅓ cup butter
  ⅓ cup diced potatoes
  ⅓ cup diced carrots
  ⅓ cup diced turnips

  2   cups fish broth, or 2 cups chicken broth or bottled clam juice
  1   eight-ounce can of Vienna sausage, sausages sliced into 1-inch-long pieces
  ½ cup diced ham
  2   tablespoons all-purpose flour
  2   hard-boiled eggs, sliced
  1   red pepper, sliced

Marinate fish chunks in mixture of lemon juice, salt and pepper for 15 minutes. In a medium skillet, melt butter and brown fish for 15 minutes. Add potatoes, carrots and turnips. Add broth. Cover and simmer for 10 minutes. Add sausage and ham. If necessary, season again with salt and pepper. Thicken sauce with flour.

On a flat surface, roll out half the pastry dough and shape it to fit a pie plate. Transfer mixture to fill pastry. Garnish with egg and pepper slices. Roll out the rest of the dough and cover the pie with it, pressing the edges to seal in the mixture. Prick the pastry with fork to let off steam. Bake in a preheated 350° F oven about 15 minutes or until pastry is browned and filling is hot.

Serves 4.

Escabeche • Sweet-and-Sour Fish

    2 pounds red snapper (sea bass,
       bluefish or carp may be
       substituted)
salt to taste
    1 cup white vinegar
    1 cup water
    ½ cup sugar
    4 tablespoons vegetable or corn
       oil
    2 cups diced bean curd (sold in
       Oriental food stores)
    6 tablespoons minced garlic
    1 cup chopped onion
    4 tablespoons ginger, sliced
       julienne-style
    2 cups sliced mushrooms
    1 cup bell pepper cut in strips
    1 tablespoon sifted flour

Clean fish and slit open. Season with salt inside and out. Mix vinegar, water, sugar and salt for sweet-sour taste. Set aside.

In a medium skillet, heat oil and fry fish and bean curd. Remove both from pan and set aside. In the same skillet, sauté garlic until light brown, then onion until transparent. Add ginger. Add the vinegar mixture. When the mixture boils, add fried fish, bean curd pieces, mushrooms and pepper, and flour to thicken. Cover the skillet and simmer for 5 minutes. Serve hot.

Serves 4.

Lapu-Lapu with Tausi
• Grouper with Black Bean Sauce

  1   pound grouper or red snapper
      fillets
  1   teaspoon minced ginger
  1   cup water
salt and freshly ground pepper to
      taste
  4   tablespoons cornstarch,
      dissolved in ⅓ cup water
 ½ cup diced bean curd
  1   tablespoon minced scallion
  1   tablespoon minced ginger
  4   tablespoons tausi (black beans;
      sold in Oriental food stores)
1½ cups water
  3   onions, cut in wedges
  3   tomatoes, cut in wedges
  1   teaspoon sesame oil

Soak the fillets and ginger in 1 cup water for 20 minutes. Remove fillets and season with salt and pepper. Roll in cornstarch-water mixture. In a medium skillet, heat oil and fry the fillets until light brown on both sides. Remove and set aside. In the same skillet, fry the bean curd until light brown. Add scallion and ginger and sauté lightly, adding the black beans and water. Thicken the mixture with cornstarch, stirring vigorously. Return fish fillets to pan, and add onions and tomatoes. Bring to a boil, then lower heat and simmer for 5 minutes. Sprinkle with sesame oil before serving. Serve hot.

Serves 2.

Paksiw Na Apahap • Fish Stew

1 pound sea bass, cut into
   serving pieces (mullet, bluefish
   or porgy may be substituted)
½ cup apple cider vinegar
¼ cup ginger, sliced in ⅛-inch
   pieces lengthwise

salt or patis to taste
1 hot green pepper
1 tablespoon vegetable or corn
   oil
½ cup water

Place dressed fish in enamelware or nonaluminum pot. Add vinegar, ginger, salt or patis and pepper. Cover and bring to boil. Add oil and water. Turn off heat as soon as the mixture boils again.

Serves 2–4.

Sinigang Na Isda • Boiled Fish

8 cups water
½ cup lemon juice
1 cup chopped onion
2 cups diced ripe tomatoes
2 cups radishes, left whole
2 pounds sea bass or bluefish
   (shelled shrimps, fresh

croaker, whitefish or squid
may be substituted), cut into
fillets
3 long, fresh hot green peppers
1½ pounds watercress or spinach
patis or salt and pepper to taste

In a saucepan, bring to a boil water, lemon juice, onion and tomatoes. Simmer for 15 minutes. Add radishes and fish and bring to a boil. Simmer till radishes are tender yet crisp. Add the hot peppers and watercress or spinach. Add patis or salt and pepper to taste.

Serves 4–6.

Guisadong Talaba • Sautéed Oysters

2 tablespoons cooking oil
1 teaspoon minced garlic
½ cup chopped onion
½ cup cubed red ripe tomatoes
2 cups shelled oysters
salt or patis and freshly ground
      pepper to taste.

Heat oil in a skillet. Sauté garlic until light brown, then onion until transparent. Add tomatoes and cook for 3 minutes. Add oysters. Simmer for another 10 minutes. Season with salt or patis and freshly ground pepper to taste.

Serves 4.

Ginataang Kuhol • Snails in Coconut Milk

1 pound fresh snails
2 cups coconut milk (sold in Oriental food stores)
1 teaspoon salt

1 tablespoon ginger root, cut into julienne strips
1 cup coconut cream (sold in Oriental food stores)

Wash snails thoroughly. Put snails in a pot with water to cover. Set aside for 5 minutes. Gently tap and break the narrow end of each snail to loosen the meat. Remove from shell and wash. In a medium pot, place the snails and the coconut milk. Simmer for 15 minutes over moderate heat. Add salt and ginger. Add coconut cream. Lower heat. Do not stir. Simmer for 5 more minutes. Serve hot.

Serves 4.

Kilawing Hipon • Shrimp Vinaigrette

1 pound shrimps, shelled, deveined and split in half
1 cup apple cider vinegar
3 tablespoons vegetable or corn oil

1½ tablespoons minced garlic
1 cup chopped onion
1 cup radish cut into strips
salt and freshly ground pepper to taste

Soak the shrimps in vinegar for 40 minutes. In a medium skillet, heat oil and sauté garlic, onion and radish. Add shrimps and vinegar. Season with salt and pepper to taste. Bring the mixture to a boil. Serve hot.

Serves 2.

Ginataang Hipon • Shrimp in Coconut Milk

2 cups coconut milk (sold in Oriental food stores)
2 pounds shrimps, shelled and deveined
1 cup water

salt and freshly ground pepper to taste
1 cup pepper leaves or any green leafy vegetable in season

In a medium pot, bring coconut milk and water to a boil. Add shrimps. Season with salt and pepper. Add pepper leaves just before turning off heat. Serve hot.

Serves 4.

Rebosadong Hipon • Fried Shrimp

1 pound fresh large shrimps
2 tablespoons lemon juice

Marinade

⅓ cup apple cider vinegar
10 peppercorns, crushed
1½ tablespoons minced garlic
½ teaspoon salt

Batter

1 cup all-purpose flour
¼ cup water
¼ cup evaporated milk
¼ teaspoon freshly ground pepper
¾ teaspoon salt
1 teaspoon baking powder
2 tablespoons anatto water (see page 204)

2 cups cooking oil

Shell the shrimps, leaving the tails. Slit open. Devein. Rub with lemon juice. Marinate the shrimps for 1 to 2 hours.

Combine batter ingredients and beat until smooth. Dip each shrimp in batter. In a large skillet, heat oil. Fry shrimps until golden brown. Drain.

Serves 2.

Rellenong Hipon • Stuffed Shrimps

- 12 very large shrimps or prawns
- 12 tablespoons ground pork or ham
- 1 tablespoon minced scallion
- 1 cup grated carrots
- 2 tablespoons minced fresh mushrooms
- 2 eggs, slightly beaten
- 4 tablespoons cornstarch
- salt and freshly ground pepper to taste
- 12 strips bacon

Shell the shrimps, leaving the tails on. Slit the back of each and devein. Combine ground pork or ham, scallion, carrots and mushrooms in a bowl. Mix the eggs and cornstarch and combine with the ground pork mixture. Season with salt and pepper to taste. Fill each shrimp with the mixture and wrap with a strip of bacon. Fry. Drain and serve hot.

Serves 4.

Laing • Shrimp in Coconut Milk

1 pound shrimps, finely
   chopped
meat from 2 small coconuts, grated
1 onion, chopped
1 teaspoon salt
10 to 15 spinach or lettuce leaves
2 cups coconut milk
2 hot green peppers

Combine shrimps, coconut, onion and salt. Spoon mixture into each vegetable leaf and wrap mixture. Arrange in pot and pour 1 cup coconut milk over wrapped mixture. Cover and simmer for about 20 minutes. When almost done, add 1 more cup of coconut milk and hot peppers. Continue cooking until sauce is thick.

Serves 3.

Gambas • Piquant Shrimp

1 pound medium-size shrimp
5 cloves garlic, minced
¼ cup olive oil
½ tablespoon lemon juice
½ cup white wine
1 tablespoon hot chili sauce
1 to 2 tablespoons bread crumbs
green olives for garnish

Prepare Spanish tomato sauce (see recipe, page 202). Set aside. Shell and devein shrimps. Set aside.

Brown garlic in olive oil. Add shrimps, lemon juice, wine and hot chili sauce. Add 3 tablespoons Spanish tomato sauce. Cook for another minute. Thicken sauce with bread crumbs. Serve hot over white rice, garnished with olives.

Serves 2–4.

Alimango Sa Tausi • Crabs in Black Bean Sauce

The crab commonly used for this recipe in the Philippines is a large, green, aggressive crab that can measure 8 inches across the back of its shell and weigh almost 3 pounds. Its claws are enormous, and at the market, the claws are usually tied with rattan fibers. This crab has almost a dozen regional names in various Philippine dialects but is generally called either a mud or mangrove crab in English because of its habitat. It is found in the Indo-Pacific from Hawaii to East Africa and from Japan to Australia. In regions where it is not available, the best-tasting local crabs can be used.

3 or 4 large crabs
  1 head garlic, minced
  2 tablespoons cooking oil
  ½ cup sliced onion
  ¼ cup fresh ginger sliced into
      thin strips
  ½ cup sliced ripe tomatoes
8-ounce can black bean sauce
  ¼ cup vinegar
  2 cups water
salt and freshly ground pepper to
      taste

Clean whole crabs and remove pincers. Remove shells and set aside. Cut crabs into two crosswise. Remove fat from shells; set aside fat and discard shells.

Sauté garlic in oil till brown, add onion and ginger and then tomatoes. Simmer for about 3 minutes. Add the black beans and then the vinegar. Add crabs and crabs' fat and simmer a few minutes. Add water, salt and pepper and cook, covered, stirring occasionally, till crabs are pink and thoroughly cooked. Serve hot.

Serves 2.

Rellenong Alimango • Stuffed Crabs

6 crabs, boiled in 2 quarts of
water and 2 cups of white
vinegar until their shells turn
red
1 cup diced potatoes
3 tablespoons vegetable or corn
oil
½ cup minced onion
1 cup fresh chopped tomatoes
salt and freshly ground pepper to
taste
3 eggs, beaten
½ cup bread crumbs

Remove crabmeat from shells. Flake evenly. Set aside. Fry potatoes in oil in a medium skillet. Remove from pan and set aside. Sauté onion and tomatoes for 2 minutes. Add crabmeat and potatoes. Season with salt and pepper. Set aside.

Clean the crab shells. Moisten with beaten eggs and fill with the mixture. Pack each shell firmly. Dust the top of stuffing with bread crumbs and dip in beaten eggs. Fry bottom side down in hot oil. Baste top with hot fat until top puffs up and turns golden brown. Drain and serve hot.

Serves 6.

Lumpiang Alimango • Crab Egg Roll

  1 cup sotanghon (bean thread
    noodles) or vermicelli cut into
    2-inch lengths
  1 6-ounce package frozen
    crabmeat
  ¼ pound ground pork
  ½ cup chopped dried Chinese
    mushrooms, soaked for 1 hour
    in water before chopping
    (discard stems)
  ½ cup scallions
  1 teaspoon patis or salt
  ½ teaspoon salt
  ⅛ teaspoon ground pepper
  ½ cup vegetable oil
 10 egg roll wrappers (see recipe
    page 24), or use 1 package
    wonton wrapper, sold in
    Oriental stores

Let noodles soak in water for 10 to 15 minutes. Drain. Except for oil, combine all ingredients for filling. Divide mixture into ten parts. Place each part in an egg roll wrapper and seal, envelop-style, taking care to moisten sides with water to seal securely.

Heat the oil in a wok or pan and fry the egg rolls until golden brown on all sides. Drain rolls. Divide each one into four pieces and serve with sweet-sour sauce (see page 202).

Serves 4.

Rellenong Pusit • Stuffed Squid

1½ pounds squid, fresh or frozen
½ cup soy sauce
1 tablespoon apple cider vinegar
salt and freshly ground pepper to
    taste
2 tablespoons garlic, minced
3 tablespoons vegetable or corn
    oil

⅓ cup finely minced onion
⅓ cup minced tomatoes
¼ pound ground pork
1 cup grated carrots
1 egg, beaten
1 cup sifted flour
1 teaspoon salt

Pull out and discard cellophanelike backbone and jawlike bone on the mouth of the squid. Wash individually. Cook squid in mixture of soy sauce, vinegar, salt, pepper and 1 tablespoon garlic for 5 minutes. Set aside.

Sauté 1 tablespoon garlic, onion and tomatoes in 1 tablespoon of oil. Add pork seasoned with salt and pepper. Stir fry for 5 minutes. Add carrots, stir frying for 2 more minutes. Remove mixture from fire. Cool.

Loosely stuff each squid with the pork mixture at the base of the head. Secure each opening with a toothpick. Dip each squid in the mixture of beaten egg, flour and salt. Fry stuffed squid in 2 tablespoons of oil for 5 minutes in a covered pan. Serve with sweet-sour sauce (see page 202).

Serves 4.

Tinolang Tulya • Clam Stew

3 cups shelled clams
1 cup unripe papaya or wintermelon, cut into 2-inch pieces
5 cups water

2 pieces ginger-root strips, cut julienne-style
salt or patis and freshly ground pepper to taste
1 pound spinach or watercress

Leave the clams in a bowl of water for 10 minutes. In a medium saucepan, bring the water and ginger to a boil. Add the clams and fruit and simmer for 15 minutes or until clams are tender. Season with salt or patis and pepper to taste. Turn off heat and add spinach or watercress. Serve hot.

Serves 4–6.

Estofadong Tulya • Clams with Burnt-Sugar Sauce

3 cups clam meat
½ cup apple cider vinegar
1 teaspoon freshly ground pepper
1 bay leaf
¼ cup cooking oil

1 tablespoon crushed garlic
1 onion, chopped
½ cup bread crumbs
2 teaspoons salt
½ teaspoon sugar

Marinate clams in vinegar, pepper and bay leaf for 40 minutes. In a large skillet, heat oil and sauté garlic until brown and onion until transparent before adding clams. Simmer until clams are tender. Add bread crumbs and salt and sugar. Serve hot.

Serves 4–6.

Kilawing Talaba # 1 • Oysters Vinaigrette

1 cup shelled oysters

Marinade

1 cup apple cider vinegar
1 cup minced red onion
1 cup minced shallots
1½ tablespoons minced garlic
salt and freshly ground pepper to
      taste

Marinate oysters for 2 hours. In a medium pot, bring the whole mixture to a boil, then remove from heat. Serve hot.

Serves 4.

Kilawing Talaba # 2 • Marinated Oysters

1 cup shelled oysters (reserve
      shells)
1 tablespoon finely minced garlic
2 tablespoons finely minced
      shallots
½ cup apple cider vinegar
salt and freshly ground pepper to
      taste

Marinate all ingredients overnight. Serve cold on empty oyster shells.

Serves 4.

9
Noodle Dishes

Noodles symbolize prosperity, long life and good luck—and the longer the noodle the better. That is why noodles generally are not broken or cut when a dish is being prepared. Noodles come in many varieties: *bihon,* rice or flour; *sotanghon,* bean; *canton,* egg; *misua,* vermicelli. Most of these varieties are available in America in food markets and Oriental stores.

Pansit is the generic term for noodle dishes of which there seem to be endless varieties. Though the origin of *pansit* is Chinese, Pansit Malabon and Pansit Luglug are strictly Filipino. Pansit Malabon is a noodle version of paella, prepared with oysters, shrimps, pork pieces, boiled eggs, Chinese celery and rice noodles. The mélange is seasoned with patis (fish sauce), black pepper, garlic and *calamansi* (the limelike native citrus fruit). It is topped with an astonishingly bright orange sauce made from shrimp juice, anatto seeds and pork rind. Pansit Luglug is a similar dish but moister in consistency.

The noodle dishes are simple to cook, but it is very important not to oversoak or overcook them. Noodles such as sotanghon and bihon require soaking; others, like misua, do not.

Pancit Guisado • Sautéed Vegetable with Noodles

10 dried Chinese mushrooms, soaked in warm water 1 hour or longer
½ pound pork, boiled and cut into ⅛-by-⅛-inch strips
5 cups water
3 bay leaves
1 cup quartered onion
1 tablespoon peppercorns
1 pound rice stick noodles
2 tablespoons finely minced garlic
1 cup minced onion
4 tablespoons corn or vegetable oil
1 cup Chinese dried pork sausage, cut crosswise into ⅛-inch slices

3 cups reserved broth
1 cup cabbage, cut julienne-style and cut again in half
1 cup carrots, cut julienne-style and cut again in half
¼ cup scallions
½ cup coriander leaves
1 teaspoon sesame oil
2 cups snow peas
2 cups cooked flaked chicken
½ pound shrimps, shelled and deveined
½ cup finely cut scallions
6 lemon wedges
2 hard-boiled eggs, sliced crosswise
soy sauce and pepper to taste

Drain mushrooms well and squeeze to extract most of the excess water. Chop and set aside. Boil pork in a mixture of 5 cups water, bay leaves, onion and peppercorns. When pork is tender, remove and cut into ⅛-by-⅛-inch strips. Set aside and save the broth.

Blanch rice stick noodles. Strain noodles and set aside.

In a wok or large saucepan, sauté garlic and onions in oil till transparent. Stir in Chinese sausage. Bring to a boil and add the 3 cups of reserved broth. Add cabbage, carrots, ¼ cup scallions and coriander and cook till done. Add noodles and sesame oil. Cook for 10 minutes. Stir in snow peas, pork, mushrooms, chicken and shrimps. Cook for 3 more minutes over low heat. Arrange on a large serving platter, sprinkle with ½ cup scallions and garnish with lemon wedges and sliced eggs. Add soy sauce and pepper to taste.

Serves 8.

Sotanghon • Chicken Vermicelli

    1   2½- to 3-pound chicken
    2   bay leaves
    1   teaspoon peppercorns
    1   cup onion, minced
    1   tablespoon finely minced garlic
    ½   cup minced onion
    3   tablespoons cooking oil
    ½   cup dried Chinese mushrooms
        (soak in 2 cups water, drain
        and add liquid to chicken
        broth)
    ½   cup anatto water (see page 204)
    ½   cup carrots, cut julienne-style
        and then in half
    ½   cup leeks, cut julienne-style
        and then in half
    ¼   cup celery, cut julienne-style
        and then in half
    ½   pound sotanghon noodles,
        also known as vermicelli (bean
        threads), soaked in water and,
        when soft, cut into 6-inch
        lengths
patis or salt and pepper to taste

In a stockpot, boil chicken, bay leaves, peppercorns and 1 cup onion. Set aside and let cool. Strain broth through a sieve. Set aside. Remove all flesh from the boiled chicken. Discard the skin and cut chicken meat into thin strips.

In a wok or frying pan, sauté garlic and ½ cup onion in oil until transparent. Stir in chicken. Add anatto water and 3 cups chicken broth and bring to boil over high heat. Stir in carrots, leeks and celery. Add sotanghon noodles. Add patis or salt and pepper to taste.

Serves 6–8.

Pancit Canton • Sautéed Egg Noodle–Cantonese Style

½ pound pork, cubed
1 chicken breast
4 cups water
4 tablespoons vegetable or corn oil
2 tablespoons minced garlic
½ cup chopped onion
1 tablespoon salt
½ pound shrimps, shelled, deveined and cut lengthwise
½ cup Chinese sausage, sliced into ⅛-inch-thick pieces
1 tablespoon pepper
1 tablespoon patis or salt
2 cups cauliflower (divided into flowerets)
2 cups snow peas
2 cups cabbage, sliced into inch strips
1 cup diced carrots
1 cup sliced celery
¼ cup diced scallions (reserve some for garnish)
2 tablespoons soy sauce
1 tablespoon sesame oil
12 ounces Cantonese noodles (egg noodles)

In a stockpot, boil pork and chicken breast in 4 cups water. When tender, remove from pot and slice into small pieces, about ½-inch strips. Reserve 3 cups broth.

In a frying pan, heat oil and sauté garlic till brown; add onion and cook till transparent. Season with salt. Stir in pork, chicken, shrimps, Chinese sausage, pepper and patis or salt. Simmer for 20 minutes. Add reserved broth and vegetables. Season with soy sauce and sesame oil. Add noodles and cook till done. Season with patis or salt and pepper to taste. Top with scallions.

Serves 4.

Bam-I • Soup Noodles with Pork and Chicken

3 tablespoons finely minced
   garlic
¼ cup chopped onion
3 tablespoons cooking oil
3 tablespoons patis or 1 teaspoon
   salt
3 cups chicken broth
½ cup chopped mushrooms
½ pound pork loin, cooked and
   cut into serving pieces
one 2-pound boned chicken breast,
   boiled and diced
½ cup celery cut into fine strips
½ cup sweet peas
1 pound sotanghon or bean
   thread noodles
½ teaspoon pepper
¼ cup scallions
   salt and pepper to taste

Sauté garlic and onion in oil. Add patis or salt, broth, mushrooms, pork, chicken, celery and peas and bring to a boil. Add sotanghon noodles and continue boiling until noodles are transparent. Season with salt and pepper to taste and add scallions just before serving.

Serves 3.

Sotanghon Bola-Bola • Noodles with Meatballs

½ cup ground pork
¼ cup chopped onion
1 egg
1 tablespoon flour
1 tablespoon salt
¼ teaspoon pepper
2 tablespoons oil
3 tablespoons minced garlic
3 tablespoons sliced onion
2 cups chicken or beef broth
1½ pounds sotanghon or bean noodles, soaked in 1 cup water*
2 tablespoons soy sauce
¼ cup diced scallions or green onions

Combine pork, onion, egg, flour, salt and pepper and form into balls about 1 inch in diameter. Sauté garlic and onion. Add broth and bring to a boil. Add meatballs one at a time and cook until meat is done. Add the sotanghon and cook for about 10 minutes. Season with soy sauce and more pepper to taste. Sprinkle with scallions just before serving. Serve hot.

Serves 4.

---

*Misua (threadlike noodles) or vermicelli can also be used. This is called Bola-Bolang Misua.

Pancit Luglug • Rice Noodles with Shrimp Sauce

2 pounds shelled shrimps
  (reserve shells)
1 cup anatto water (see page 204)
½ pound pork loin, boiled and
  sliced into 1-by-1-inch pieces
3 tablespoons vegetable or corn
  oil
1 tablespoon finely minced garlic
1 cup finely minced onion
½ cup finely minced parsley
salt and freshly ground pepper to
  taste

4 tablespoons all-purpose flour
1 pound rice noodles (or
  spaghetti noodles)
1 cup smoked fish, finely flaked
  (or smoked oysters)
2 cups pork cracklings, pounded
  to a powder
½ cup finely minced parsley
½ cup finely minced scallions
2 hard-boiled eggs, sliced
6 lemon slices

Prepare shrimp juice by puréeing the shrimp shells in a food processor. Add ½ cup water to the purée; mix, mash and strain. (Canned shrimp bisque can be substituted.) Set aside. Prepare anatto water. Set aside.

Boil pork in enough water to cover until tender. Cube meat and set aside along with ½ cup broth.

In a large skillet, heat oil and sauté garlic and onion. Brown garlic and cook onion until transparent. Add pork cubes and shrimp. Stir gently. Add shrimp juice, parsley and salt and pepper to taste. Add anatto water and bring to a boil. Lower heat. Mix the flour with reserved ½ cup of pork broth and add to the mixture. Bring to a boil, stirring constantly. Set aside.

Boil pancit or spaghetti in 5 quarts of water until cooked. Drain. Transfer noodles to a large platter. Pour the shrimp sauce mixture on the noodles or serve in a separate bowl. Garnish with smoked fish flakes, pork cracklings, parsley, scallions, egg slices and lemon slices. Serve hot.

Serves 6–8.

Pancit Malabon • Noodle Dish from Malabon

Malabon is a town in the Philippines.

½ cup vegetable or corn oil
1 tablespoon finely minced garlic
1 cup diced tokwa or bean curd
  (sold in Oriental food stores)
½ cup diced lean pork
1 cup shelled oysters
½ cup squid, cut into rings

1 teaspoon salt
½ teaspoon freshly ground
  pepper

1 pound bihon or rice noodles
  (sold in Oriental food stores)

Sauce

2 tablespoons oil
1 tablespoon finely minced garlic
1 cup finely minced onion
2 tablespoons anatto water (see
  page 204)
2 tablespoons cornstarch
1 cup shrimp juice*
½ cup tokwa or bean curd,
  mashed
3 tablespoons patis or

Garnish

1 cup pork cracklings, pounded
  to powder
½ cup smoked fish, finely flaked
  (or smoked oysters)
½ cup finely minced scallions
lemon slices
patis or salt

In a large skillet, heat oil and sauté garlic till brown. Add bean curd, pork, oysters and squid. Set aside. In the same skillet, cook the sauce, using the leftover oil.

Heat the oil. Sauté garlic and onion. Cook till garlic is brown and onion is transparent. Add the anatto water. Dissolve the cornstarch in the shrimp juice and add to the mixture. Add the bean curd and simmer over moderate heat until the mixture is thick. Season with patis and pepper. Turn off the heat and set aside.

Soak the noodles in hot water for about 5 minutes or until soft. Drain and transfer to a platter. Pour the sauce on top. Garnish with pork cracklings, smoked fish flakes and scallions. Serve hot with lemon slices and patis or salt.

Serves 4.

---

*Shrimp juice: Purée shrimp shells in a food processor. Add ½ cup of water to the puree, mix, mash and strain. Canned shrimp bisque can also be substituted.

Pancit Miki • Noodles with Bean Sprouts

½ pound miki or Chinese egg
   noodles (flat, wide noodles,
   sold in Oriental food stores)
1 cup vegetable or corn oil (to be
   used a little at a time)
2 cups dried Chinese
   mushrooms
1 egg, slightly beaten
¼ pound lean pork, cut into
   serving strips
1 tablespoon cornstarch
1 tablespoon patis or salt
½ pound bean sprouts
1 tablespoon soy sauce
½ cup chicken stock

Cook noodles according to package directions. Stir in 1 tablespoon vegetable oil to keep the noodles from sticking together. Set aside.

Soak mushrooms in water for about 30 minutes. When they are soft and expanded, drain and slice the mushrooms thin. Set aside.

Fry the egg and cut into strips. Set aside.

Coat the pork strips with cornstarch and patis or salt. In a medium skillet, heat 2 tablespoons of oil and stir fry the pork strips. Add bean sprouts, mushrooms, soy sauce and chicken stock, stirring occasionally.

In another large skillet, heat the rest of the oil. Add the noodles and fry on both sides, turning them once. Drain on absorbent paper. Transfer the noodles to a serving platter. Pour the meat-vegetable mixture on top. Garnish with egg strips. Serve hot.

Serves 4.

Pancit Mami • Noodles in Broth

¼ pound lean pork
¼ pound chicken, whole piece
3 cups water
1 teaspoon salt
2 tablespoons vegetable or corn oil
1 tablespoon finely minced garlic
1 minced onion
salt and pepper to taste
1 pound fresh miki (rice noodles sold in Oriental food stores), or flat, wide egg noodles
2 tablespoons finely minced scallions

In a medium pot, boil pork and chicken in 3 cups water until tender. Season with salt. Remove from water and cool. Cut the pork into strips and shred the chicken. Set aside, saving 2 cups stock. In a large skillet, heat oil and sauté garlic and onion. Add pork and chicken. Add the stock. Simmer for two minutes and season with salt and pepper. Put uncooked miki in serving bowls and pour over enough of the chicken-pork broth to fill the bowls (the hot broth will cook the noodles). Garnish each bowl with minced scallions and serve hot.

Serves 4.

Pancit con Caldo • Egg-Noodle Broth

2 tablespoons vegetable or corn
   oil
1 tablespoon finely minced garlic
1 cup chopped onion
1 cup diced pork loin
2 teaspoons salt
1 tablespoon patis or salt
¼ teaspoon freshly ground
   pepper
6 cups water
½ pound miki or egg noodles
   (sold in Oriental food stores)
1 cup diced zucchini
½ cup shelled and deveined
   shrimps
2 eggs

In a large skillet, heat oil and sauté garlic and onion till garlic turns brown and onion transparent. Add diced pork. Season with salt, patis if used and pepper. Add water. Bring the whole mixture to a boil and add the noodles. Simmer for 5 to 8 minutes until the noodles are tender, stirring occasionally. Add zucchini and shrimps. Simmer for 3 more minutes. Drop in the raw eggs without beating. Bring the broth to a boil and serve hot.

Serves 4.

Pancit Butong • Coconut Noodles

- 2 tablespoons vegetable or corn oil
- 1 tablespoon finely minced garlic
- ⅓ cup sliced onion
- ⅓ cup sliced tomatoes
- 1 cup tofu (bean curd), fried and cut into 1-by-2-inch strips
- 2 tablespoons soy sauce
- 1 teaspoon salt
- 4 cups chicken stock
- 1 cup dried mushrooms, soaked for 30 minutes and cut into strips
- 3 young coconuts, meat cut into strips
- 1 green pepper, cut into strips
- 1 red pepper, cut into strips
- 3 sprigs parsley

In a medium pot, heat oil and sauté garlic until light brown, onion until transparent and tomatoes until soft. Add fried tofu or bean curd, soy sauce and salt. Add chicken stock and mushrooms. Cover and simmer over moderate heat for 10 minutes. Add coconut. Cook until tender. Add green and red pepper and parsley. Serve hot.

Serves 6.

Pancit Molo • Philippine Wonton Soup

Filling

1 cup ground pork
½ cup shrimps, shelled and chopped
½ cup finely chopped onion
2 egg yolks
¼ cup finely sliced scallions
2 teaspoons finely minced garlic
½ cup finely minced water chestnuts
1 teaspoon salt
¼ teaspoon pepper

Combine all ingredients and blend well. Set aside.

Wrapper (can also be bought ready-made at Oriental food stores)

2 cups all-purpose flour
¼ teaspoon salt
3 egg yolks
¼ cup water

Sift flour and salt together. Add the yolks and knead with fingers. Gradually add water and continue kneading until dough is elastic and smooth. Roll out on a floured board until paper thin. Cut into triangles, with sides of each triangle measuring about 3 inches. Scoop 1 teaspoon filling onto each wrapper and fold two corners in. Fold and press third corner to seal like a pouch. (When using ready-made wrappers, fold two corners opposite each other and then the two others to seal like a pouch.)

Broth

one 3-pound chicken
15 cups water
 2 tablespoons finely minced
   garlic
 1 cup finely chopped onion
 2 tablespoons vegetable or corn
   oil
 1 cup shrimps, shelled and
   deveined
patis or salt and freshly ground
   pepper
 ½ cup finely chopped scallions

Boil chicken in water till tender. Remove meat from bones, cut into serving pieces and set aside chicken and broth.

Sauté garlic and onion in oil. Garlic is done when light brown and onion when transparent. Add the chicken, broth, sautéed mixture and shrimps. Season with patis or salt and pepper to taste. Bring to a boil. Drop the wrapped stuffing into the broth and cook for 10 minutes. Garnish with scallions.

Serves 4.

Misua con Patola • Noodles with Zucchini

- 2 tablespoons cooking oil
- 1 tablespoon finely minced garlic
- ¼ cup finely minced onion
- 2 medium zucchini, sliced in rings
- 2 cups chicken stock
- 1 packet misua (threadlike noodles sold in Oriental stores, or vermicelli may be substituted)

salt and freshly ground pepper to taste

In a medium pot, heat oil and sauté garlic and onion. Cook until garlic is brown and onion transparent. Add the zucchini. Add the chicken stock and bring the whole mixture to a boil. Add misua and stir well. Season with salt and pepper. Serve hot.

Serves 2.

Misua • Threadlike Noodle Soup

   1 small bundle or 2 ounces misua
     (sold in Oriental food stores)
   2 tablespoons vegetable or corn
     oil
   1 tablespoon finely minced garlic
   ¼ cup finely minced onion
   1 cup ground pork loin
   4 cups water
salt and freshly ground pepper to
     taste
   3 eggs, beaten
   ¼ cup chopped scallions

Break noodles into 3-inch lengths. In a medium saucepan, heat oil. Sauté garlic
and onion; add pork and brown. Add water, salt and pepper. Bring to a quick
boil. Slowly pour in raw, beaten eggs. Add misua and simmer for 10 minutes.
Serve hot, garnished with scallions.

Serves 4.

Lang-Lang
• Noodles with Chicken, Shrimp and Snow Peas

½ cup dried Chinese mushrooms
1 small package sotanghon (bean-thread noodles, sold in Oriental food stores)
one 2- to 3-pound chicken, cut into serving pieces
2 cups water
6 cloves garlic, crushed

2 tablespoons oil
¼ cup chopped onion
½ pound shrimps, shelled and deveined
2 tablespoons patis or 1 tablespoon salt
¼ teaspoon pepper
¼ pound snow peas

Soak mushrooms and sotanghon noodles separately until both are soft. Cook chicken with water in a covered pan until the meat starts to fall off the bones. Set aside. Fry garlic in oil and set aside half for garnish. To pan with chicken and broth, add half the garlic, onion, shrimp, salt and pepper. Bring to a boil and simmer for 10 minutes. Add sotanghon noodles and mushrooms and continue cooking for 5 to 10 minutes. Add snow peas and cook for another 5 minutes. Before serving, sprinkle with the reserved fried garlic.

Serves 4.

Laksa • Bean Noodles with Vegetables

Laksa literally means "ten thousand." This dish is given the name because it uses an assortment of vegetables.

3 tablespoons vegetable or corn oil
1 tablespoon finely minced garlic
1 cup finely minced onion
½ cup cubed pork butt
1 cup shelled shrimps (use shells for shrimp juice)
1½ cups shrimp juice or canned shrimp bisque*
2 cups string beans cut into ½-inch pieces
one 10-ounce package frozen lima beans

1 eggplant, diced and peeled
1 cup diced squash
2 cups squash leaves or any green leafy vegetable
2 cups sotanghon, whole or cut into 1-inch pieces, soaked in water and drained
3 tablespoons patis or 1 tablespoon salt
1 teaspoon freshly ground pepper

In a large skillet, heat oil and sauté garlic and onion. Cook until garlic is brown and onion transparent. Add pork, shrimps and shrimp juice or bisque. Simmer until pork is cooked. Add string beans and lima beans. Add eggplant, squash and squash leaves. Add sotanghon. Simmer over moderate heat for 8 minutes. Season with patis or salt and pepper. Serve hot.

Serves 4.

*Shrimp juice is preferable. To make this, purée shrimp shells in a food processor. Add ½ cup water to the purée, mix, mash and strain.

Fritong Pinsec • Fried Wonton

Filling

½ pound ground pork
½ pound shrimps, shelled,
  deveined and chopped
½ cup chopped scallions
1 cup finely chopped bamboo
  shoots (canned)
½ cup chopped dried Chinese
  mushrooms, soaked in water
  for 1 hour before chopping and
  stems discarded
½ cup finely chopped and
  drained water chestnuts
1 egg
2 tablespoons cornstarch
salt and freshly ground pepper to
  taste
2 tablespoons soy sauce
½ cup cooking oil

Combine all ingredients except cooking oil in a mixing bowl. Put 1 tablespoon of the mixture on each wrapper (see recipe that follows). Seal wrapper by folding diagonally. Deep fry in cooking oil until golden brown on all sides. Serve with sweet-sour sauce (recipe follows).

Wonton Wrappers (ready-made wrappers can be bought at Oriental food stores)

2 cups all-purpose flour
2 eggs, beaten
2 to 4 tablespoons water

Place flour on a flat surface. Make well in the middle and drop eggs and water in well. Mix the ingredients in the center thoroughly, and quickly work in the flour. Knead the mixture until dough is smooth and elastic. With rolling pin, roll out dough on floured board till paper thin. Cut into 3-by-3-inch squares.

Sweet-and-Sour Sauce

2	cups water
½	cup catsup
1	tablespoon Worcestershire sauce
4	tablespoons sugar
2 to 4	tablespoons white vinegar
3	tablespoons cornstarch

Combine all ingredients. Bring to a boil and simmer for about 10 minutes.

Serves 4.

Bola-Bolang Misua • Vermicelli with Fish Balls

    1   pound sea bass
    5   tablespoons all-purpose flour
    1   tablespoon salt
    2   tablespoons finely minced
        scallions
    ½   cup finely minced onion
    2   tablespoons cooking oil
    1   tablespoon finely minced garlic
    3   cups water
    3   tablespoons patis or salt
    1-pound packet misua (sold in
        Oriental food stores, or
        vermicelli may be substituted)
    salt and freshly ground pepper to
        taste
    1   cup finely chopped spinach

Clean the fish. Steam in sieve over boiling water for about 10 minutes or until flaky. Flake fish, then set aside. Combine the flour, salt, scallions and half the minced onion. Mix with the fish flakes and form into small balls about 1 inch in diameter.

In a medium saucepan, heat the oil. Sauté garlic and the rest of the onion. Garlic is done when light brown, onion when transparent. Add water and bring to a boil. Season with patis or salt. Add the fish balls and simmer over moderate heat for 3 minutes. Add misua or vermicelli and simmer for 5 minutes. Season with salt and pepper. Add spinach and cook for another 2 minutes. Serve hot.

Serves 4.

10
Vegetable Dishes

Like the Chinese, the Filipinos cook their vegetables with meat and other ingredients. In fact, a plain vegetable dish is hard to find. Vegetable dishes are simmered with beef, chicken, fish or shrimp and often with soy sauce, lemon juice, patis (fish sauce), vinegar, garlic, onions and tomatoes. The method of cooking vegetable dishes is similar to the methods for cooking meat and fish, and the point at which a vegetable dish becomes a main dish and vice versa depends on the proportion of meat to vegetable.

Many vegetables and fruits that are common in the Philippines are never seen in the United States. However, plenty of domestic vegetables can be successfully substituted. Some of these are available in most large markets; others have to be sought out in Hispanic or Oriental stores. As the American diet continues to diversify, more vegetables that were formerly considered exotic will find their way to local food markets.

Pinakbet • Sautéed Vegetable with Shrimp Paste

This dish is similar to the French ratatouille.

1	tablespoon finely minced garlic
½	cup finely chopped onion
2	tablespoons vegetable or corn oil
¾	pound pork, sliced into 1-inch cubes
5	½-inch-thick slices fresh ginger
4	ripe tomatoes, cubed
½	cup sautéed-type bagoong (available in Oriental stores)
½	cup water
3	medium-size eggplants, cut into 2-inch cubes
2	cups bitter melon, cut into 2-inch lengths (scrape out the soft center and the seeds, then cut into 2-inch-long pieces), zucchini can be substituted

10-ounce package frozen okra
10-ounce package frozen lima
  beans
salt and pepper to taste

Sauté garlic and onion in hot oil until onion is transparent. Add pork. Stir and cook for 15 minutes. Add ginger and tomatoes and cook for 10 minutes. Add bagoong and stir for 3 minutes. Add water and bring to a boil. Add eggplant, bitter melon, okra and lima beans. Simmer for 15 minutes. Season with salt and pepper if desired.

Serves 4.

Lumpiang Ubod • Hearts of Palm Spring Rolls

Filling

3	tablespoons vegetable or corn oil
1	tablespoon finely minced garlic
½	cup finely minced onion
2	cups hearts of palm, cut julienne-style
½	pound deveined, shelled shrimp (minced)
½	pound boiled pork, sliced thin (⅛- by ⅛-inch pieces)
1	cup green beans, sliced julienne-style
	salt and freshly ground pepper to taste

Sauté garlic and onion in oil. When garlic browns and onion becomes transparent, add hearts of palm and cook until tender. Stir in shrimp and pork. Cook until tender. Add green beans and simmer for 3 minutes. Season with salt and pepper.

Wrap 3 tablespoons of this mixture in a ready-made spring roll wrapper (available in Oriental food stores) or make your own.

Wrappers

3	eggs
2	tablespoons vegetable or corn oil
1	cup cornstarch
½	teaspoon salt
14	lettuce leaves
1½	cups water
1	cup finely crushed peanuts

Beat eggs thoroughly; add oil. Stir in cornstarch and salt until dissolved. Add water and mix well. Heat omelet pan and pour in a thin coating of batter to make egg roll. Set aside. Repeat until you have made 14 or more wrappers.

Lay out the spring roll wrappers on a flat surface. Place a lettuce leaf extending over border of wrapper. Add 3 tablespoons of filling. Roll and fold one end. Leave the other end open to show the lettuce leaf. Serve without further cooking, garnished with sauce and crushed peanuts (brush sauce on egg roll and sprinkle with crushed peanuts).

Sauce

½	cup sugar
2	cups water
3	tablespoons soy sauce
3½	teaspoons salt
⅛	teaspoon freshly ground pepper
2	tablespoons cornstarch

Combine all ingredients in a saucepan. Cook, stirring constantly, over high heat until the sauce thickens. Let cool.

Yield: About 15 rolls.

Lumpia • Vegetable Spring Roll

Filling

2 tablespoons vegetable oil for
sautéing
1 tablespoon finely minced garlic
½ cup finely minced onion
½ pound boiled pork, sliced into
⅛- by ⅛-inch squares
½ cup shrimps, shelled, deveined
and chopped
2 cups chicken broth
1 cup cabbage, finely shredded
4 carrots, diced

3 medium-size potatoes, diced
1 sweet potato, diced
¼ pound green beans, sliced
diagonally
2 cups boiled chick peas
2 tablespoons soy sauce
lettuce leaves
2 tablespoons finely chopped
parsley
1 cup ground roast peanuts

Wrappers

See Lumpiang Ubod, page 180.

Fresh Lumpia Sauce

See Lumpiang Ubod, page 180.

Heat oil in pan and sauté garlic until light brown. Add onion. When onion turns transparent, add pork, shrimps and broth. Simmer for 20 minutes. Add cabbage, carrots, potatoes, sweet potato, green beans, chick peas and soy sauce. Cook until vegetables are tender. Set aside and let cool.

On a flat surface, spread out wrappers and line each with a lettuce leaf. Put 3 tablespoons of filling on each wrapper and sprinkle with parsley and ground peanuts before sealing. Make roll by folding one side of wrapper to seal in the filling and leave one side open so that lettuce leaf is visible. Before serving, top with Lumpia Sauce.

Serves 4.

Fried Lumpia • Fried Egg Roll

Filling

Same as Lumpia (see page 182).

Procedure

Same as Lumpia Shanghai (see page 23).

Dip

1 cup vinegar
⅛ teaspoon salt
3 cloves garlic, crushed

Mix all ingredients together.

Serves 4.

Guisadong Gulay • Sautéed Vegetable

½ pound boneless pork loin butt
3 cups water
6 cloves garlic, finely minced
½ cup minced onion
4 tomatoes, chopped
3 tablespoons cooking oil
½ pound shrimp, shelled and deveined
2 tablespoons patis or 1 tablespoon salt
¼ teaspoon freshly ground black pepper
1 cup carrots cut into bite-size pieces
1 cup broccoli cut into bite-size pieces
1 cup cabbage cut into bite-size pieces
1 cup cauliflower cut into bite-size pieces
1 cup snow peas cut into bite-size pieces

In an 8-inch saucepan, boil pork in 3 cups water; let cool and cut pork into 1-inch strips. Set aside, and reserve 1½ cups broth. In a frying pan or wok, sauté garlic, onion and tomatoes in hot oil. Cook garlic until brown before adding onion. When onion becomes transparent, add tomatoes and cook until soft. Add pork strips, shrimp, reserved pork broth and patis or salt and pepper. Bring to a boil. Add vegetables one at a time, stirring occasionally, making sure that cooking time is provided for less tender ones. Serve hot.

Serves 4–6.

Guisadong Sitao
• Sautéed String Beans or Yard-Long Beans

2 tablespoons vegetable or corn
 oil
2 tablespoons minced garlic
½ cup chopped onion
2 ripe tomatoes, cubed
½ cup pork, boiled and cut in
 thin strips
½ cup shelled and deveined
 shrimp
salt or patis and freshly ground
 pepper to taste
½ pound string beans, cut
 crosswise into 2-inch pieces

Heat oil and sauté garlic until light brown and onion until transparent. Add tomatoes and cook until soft. Stir in pork and shrimp. Add patis or salt and pepper and bring to a boil, stirring occasionally. Add string beans. Cook until beans are crisp-tender. Serve hot.

Serves 4.

Mongo Guisado • Sautéed Mung Beans

1 cup mongo (mung beans),
   soaked overnight in water
3 cups water
2 tablespoons vegetable or corn
   oil
1 teaspoon minced garlic
¼ cup chopped onion
2 ripe tomatoes, cubed
¼ cup pork, cut in 1-inch cubes
¼ cup shrimps, shelled and
   deveined
2 cups water
salt or patis and freshly ground
   pepper to taste
1 tablespoon bagoong
½ pound spinach or watercress

Boil mung beans in 3 cups of water until tender. In another pan, heat oil and sauté garlic and onion. Garlic is done when light brown and onion when transparent. Add tomatoes and cook them until soft. Add pork and cook until tender. Add shrimps and cook for additional 5 minutes. Add the boiled mung beans and 2 cups water to the sautéed mixture. Bring to a boil again. Season with salt or patis, pepper, and bagoong. Add the spinach or watercress immediately after mixture comes to a boil. Serve hot.

Serves 4.

Bulanglang • Boiled Vegetables

½ cup quartered onion
2 tomatoes, chopped
1½ teaspoons bagoong or shrimp
   paste (sold in Oriental stores)
1 cup cubed butternut squash
1 cup water
1 cup bean curd, sliced and fried
1 cup sliced zucchini
½ pound spinach

Combine onion, tomatoes, bagoong or shrimp paste and squash in a deep sauce-pan. Add water and bring to a boil. Add bean curd and zucchini. Simmer until zucchini is tender. Add spinach and cook for another 3 minutes. Serve hot.

Serves 4.

Laing • Spinach with Coconut Milk

1 pound spinach
1½ cups coconut milk
1½ teaspoons salt
1 teaspoon minced ginger root
½ cup diced pork
½ cup diced shrimps
½ cup coconut cream (sold in
   Oriental food stores)
2 hot green peppers

Chop the spinach leaves into desired lengths. Set aside. In a saucepan, combine coconut milk, salt, ginger and pork. Simmer until meat is cooked. Add shrimps and simmer for 5 minutes. Add coconut cream, hot peppers and spinach. Simmer for an additional 3 minutes. Serve hot.

Serves 4.

Mais Guisado • Sautéed Corn

    2   tablespoons cooking oil
    1   tablespoon finely minced garlic
    ¼   cup minced onion
    ½   pound shrimps, shelled,
        deveined, and cut into small
        pieces
    ½   cup chicken broth
salt or patis and freshly ground
        pepper to taste
    3   cups corn (canned, frozen or
        fresh)
    ½   pound spinach

Heat oil in a medium pot. Sauté garlic until light brown and onion until transparent. Add shrimps. Add chicken broth. Season with salt or patis and pepper. Bring to a boil. Add corn and simmer until corn is cooked. Add spinach and simmer for 3 minutes. Serve hot.

Serves 4.

Guisadong Upo • Sautéed Gourd or Zucchini

    2   tablespoons cooking oil
    1   tablespoon finely minced garlic
    1   tablespoon bagoong or shrimp
        paste (sold in Oriental stores)
salt to taste
    ½   pound shrimps, shelled and
        deveined
    2   cups upo (or zucchini)

In a medium skillet, heat oil and sauté garlic until brown. Add bagoong or shrimp paste and salt. Add shrimps and bring to a very short boil (about 4 minutes). Add upo or zucchini, cover pan and stir occasionally. Cook for about 10 minutes until upo or zucchini is tender.

Serves 4.

Rellenong Talong • Stuffed Eggplant

2   medium-size eggplants
2   eggs, beaten
2   tablespoons cooking oil
1   teaspoon finely minced garlic
½   cup finely minced onion
1   pound ground pork or beef
3   ripe tomatoes, chopped
patis or salt and freshly ground
     pepper to taste
1   cup bread crumbs
3   tablespoons vegetable or corn
     oil

Cut eggplants lengthwise into halves. Broil, skin side up, until tender. Let cool and scoop out pulp and discard. Reserve skin. Soak skin in beaten eggs. In a skillet, heat oil and sauté garlic until brown, onion until transparent. Add pork or beef and cook until brown. Add tomatoes, patis or salt and pepper to taste. Continue stirring mixture until it is not too moist. Remove from heat. Divide stuffing mixture into 4 portions and fill the four eggplant skins with it. Press to make firm and coat each with bread crumbs and beaten eggs. Heat oil and fry eggplants on one side and then the other until golden brown.

Serves 4.

Calabasang Guisado • Sautéed Squash

    2 tablespoons cooking oil
    1 tablespoon minced garlic
    ¼ cup chopped onion
    ½ cup shrimps, shelled and
       deveined
  1½ cups thinly sliced squash
    1 cup water
salt or patis and freshly ground
       pepper to taste

Heat oil. Sauté garlic until light brown and onion until transparent. Add shrimps and squash. Stir for one minute. Add water. Season with salt or patis and pepper and bring to a boil. Simmer for 3 minutes. Serve hot.

Serves 4.

Kilawin Labanos • Sautéed Radish

    6 medium-size radishes
salt
    1 clove garlic, crushed
    1 medium-size onion, sliced
    1 medium-size tomato, sliced
    1 tablespoon cooking oil
    ½ cup pork cut in strips
    ½ cup shrimps
salt and pepper
    2 tablespoons vinegar

Slice radishes very thin. Sprinkle with salt to remove bitterness. Rinse in water, drain and set aside. Sauté garlic, onion, and tomato in oil. Add pork and cook until brown. Cut shrimps lengthwise and add to sautéed pork. Simmer until done. Season with salt and pepper. Add radishes. Cover and simmer for 10 minutes. Add vinegar and more pepper and bring to a boil. Serve hot.

Serves 4.

11
Salads, Relishes and Condiments

Philippine salads are particularly appealing because of the wide variety of tropical fruits and vegetables grown in the country. The influence of the Americans in the Philippines has made salad part of the Philippine meal.

Philippine salads consist mainly of fruits and vegetables, fish or relish. Most of the ingredients are first cooked (blanched, boiled, baked or preserved in jars or bottles) before being mixed or tossed together.

At every Filipino meal is a wide variety of side dishes, to accompany and enhance the main dishes being served. The most famous of these condiments is *bagoong*, the salty shrimp paste that many Filipinos feel *must* accompany almost every meal—similar to the fondness of most Americans for having a salt shaker at the table.

Dipping Sauces

Dipping sauces are another part of almost every meal in the Philippines. Their strong accents and eye-appealing presentations enhance not only the flavor of foods but all aspects of a meal.

The sauces are created right at the table by each individual, with the ingredients provided. The table is set with tiny, saucerlike dishes for this purpose, and proportions vary according to each person's taste.

Condiments	Served with
patis and calamansi*	boiled beef
soy sauce and calamansi	meat, vegetables or noodles
bagoong and calamansi	broiled fish
vinegar and crushed garlic	broiled pork
vinegar, crushed garlic and soy sauce	roasted meat
vinegar and red pepper	fresh fish
bagoong	kare-kare or fresh green mangoes
bagoong, chopped fresh tomatoes and onions	boiled fish
bagoong and chopped coriander	broiled or fried fish

---

*Patis is fish sauce and calamansi is a limelike citrus fruit found in the Philippines. Lemons and limes can be substituted (see Chapter 1).

Ensaladang Pilipino • Philippine Salad

1 head romaine lettuce
1 cup vinaigrette sauce (see
   recipe below)
5 salted eggs (sold only in
   Philippine food stores) or
   hard-boiled eggs
5 medium-size tomatoes, sliced
salt to taste

Separate lettuce leaves into serving pieces and line salad platter with them. Pour ¼ cup vinaigrette sauce over lettuce. Peel salted or hard-boiled eggs and chop coarsely. Slice tomatoes crosswise in wedges. Arrange tomato slices over lettuce, then add eggs. Pour remaining vinaigrette sauce over top.

Serves 6.

Vinaigrette Sauce

½ cup apple cider vinegar
½ teaspoon salt
1 teaspoon sugar
¼ cup water
2 teaspoons finely minced
   parsley

Mix all ingredients and serve.

Yield: 1½ cups.

Talong At Kamatis • Eggplant and Tomato Salad

1 large eggplant
5 medium-size tomatoes,
  chopped
1 cup finely minced onion
2 tablespoons finely minced
  parsley
2 tablespoons olive oil
salt and pepper to taste

Preheat oven to 350° F. Peel eggplant and cut lengthwise into ½-inch-thick slices. Place on cookie sheet and bake until eggplant slices are tender; separate and let cool.

In a mixing bowl, combine eggplant, tomatoes, onion, parsley and oil. Add salt and pepper to taste. Serve cold.

Serves 4.

Ubod Ng Niyog • Hearts of Palm Salad

one 16-ounce can hearts of palm
1 cup finely minced onion
1 head romaine lettuce

Chop hearts of palm coarsely. Add finely minced onion and mix well. Line salad platter with romaine lettuce. Arrange hearts-of-palm mixture on top. Serve cold with vinaigrette sauce (see page 194).

Serves 4.

Burong Mustasa • Pickled Mustard Greens

3 pounds mustard greens
½ cup kosher salt or sea salt
8 cups water

Trim and separate the mustard greens. Wash in cold running water. Dry each leaf thoroughly, since moisture will cause mold. Salt the leaves, then squeeze them firmly to let out the juice. Place the leaves in a clean, dry glass jar. Pour enough water to cover the leaves and have at least 1 inch of water besides. Cover the jar tightly and store in a cool dark place for a week. This may be eaten as a side dish with fried fish.

Serves 8.

Kangkong Salad Substitute • Spinach Salad

1 pound fresh or frozen spinach
2 tomatoes, sliced
½ cup finely minced scallions
2 tablespoons patis or 1 teaspoon
   salt
½ teaspoon fresh ginger, finely
   minced (optional)
lemon wedges

In a medium saucepan, blanch the spinach. To blanch, use 2 tablespoons of water with fresh spinach and nothing when using frozen spinach. Cover the pot and cook over moderate heat for 3 minutes. Let stand and cool. Combine the tomatoes, scallions, patis or salt and ginger, if used. Mix with the spinach. Serve cold with lemon wedges.

Serves 4.

Pipino Salad • Cucumber Salad

- 2 medium-size cucumbers
- 1 teaspoon salt
- 1/8 teaspoon freshly ground pepper
- 1 tablespoon sugar
- 1 tablespoon finely minced ginger
- 1/4 cup red wine vinegar

lettuce leaves and tomato slices for garnish

Wash, thoroughly dry and slice cucumbers thin. Combine salt, pepper, sugar, ginger and red wine vinegar. Mix well with the cucumber slices. Refrigerate for an hour before serving. Serve on lettuce leaves. Garnish with tomato slices.

Serves 4.

Togue Salad • Bean Sprout Salad

- 1 pound bean sprouts
- 4 cups water
- 1 tablespoon rice wine or any white wine
- 1/2 cup chopped scallions
- 2 tablespoons soy sauce
- 2 tablespoons sesame oil

Rinse the bean sprouts thoroughly. In a medium saucepan, bring 4 cups water to a boil. Turn off heat and add the bean sprouts. Let stand for 3 minutes and drain well. Combine wine, scallions, soy sauce and sesame oil. Pour on the bean sprouts and mix well. Refrigerate for an hour or longer before serving.

Serves 4.

Achara (Relish)

This Indian-influenced melange of sweet-sour relish is a favorite in the Philippines. It is usually eaten as a side dish to accompany fried or broiled fish or meat.

1   cup apple cider vinegar
1   cup sugar
1   tablespoon salt
4   cups sauerkraut*
4   cloves garlic, sliced
    julienne-style and cut in half
1   cup carrots, sliced
    julienne-style and cut in half
1   sweet green pepper, cored,
    seeded and sliced
    julienne-style
1   sweet red pepper, cored,
    seeded and sliced
    julienne-style
¼   pound ginger, sliced
    julienne-style
1   cup finely minced onion
½   cup raisins

Bring vinegar, sugar and salt to a boil in a large saucepan. Add the rest of the ingredients, cover and turn off heat. Let cool. Transfer to sterilized jar or bottle.

Yield: About 7 cups.

---

*The original recipe calls for green papaya cut into julienne strips.

Acharang Labanos • Radish Relish

4 medium-size white radishes
2 teaspoons salt
1 cup pickle juice

Pare the radishes. Slice into thin, short pieces. Add salt and squeeze out the juice to remove the bitter taste of the radishes. Rinse in water and squeeze liquid out. Add enough pickle juice to cover the radishes. Serve with any fried or broiled fish or meat.

Yield: 10 portions.

Acharang Mais • Corn Relish

1 teaspoon salt
½ cup sugar
½ cup apple cider vinegar
1 cup cooked or canned corn
1 medium-size onion, diced
1 medium-size green pepper, diced
2 teaspoons hot pepper sauce
¼ cup finely diced pimento

Combine salt, sugar and vinegar in saucepan. Bring to a boil. Add corn, onion and green pepper and boil for 5 minutes. Stir in hot pepper sauce and pimento to taste. Refrigerate. Serve cold.

Yield: 4 cups.

Note: The following dishes are rarely eaten by themselves but as accompaniments to boiled or fried fish or meat.

Bagoong Alamang Guisado • Sautéed Shrimp Paste

4   tablespoons cooking oil
1   tablespoon finely minced garlic
½   cup finely minced onion
½   cup minced tomatoes
1   cup pork butt sliced into
     ¼-inch pieces or less
one 12-ounce jar of bagoong
     alamang or shrimp paste (sold
     in Oriental food stores)
3   tablespoons sugar
vinegar to taste

In a skillet, heat oil and sauté garlic until light brown, onion until transparent and tomatoes until soft. Stir in pork and cook until tender. Add bagoong alamang, sugar and vinegar and simmer for 10 minutes.

Yield: 2 cups.

Sarsang Lechón • Liver Sauce

one 4-ounce can liver pâté or
    spread
⅓ cup vinegar
1 cup water
⅓ cup sugar
⅓ cup bread crumbs
1 teaspoon salt
⅓ teaspoon black pepper
2 tablespoons cooking oil
1 tablespoon minced garlic
2 tablespoons finely chopped
    onion

Mix liver pâté or spread, vinegar, water, sugar, bread crumbs, salt and pepper. In a small saucepan, heat oil and sauté garlic till brown. Add onion and cook until transparent. Add liver mixture. Bring to a boil and simmer till sauce thickens to taste. Serve with roast pork or beef.

Yield: 2 cups.

Agre Dulce • Sweet-and-Sour Sauce

    2 cups water
    ½ cup catsup
    ⅓ cup sugar
    1 teaspoon salt
    1 teaspoon red-hot sauce
       (optional)
    3 tablespoons cornstarch
       dissolved in 4 tablespoons
       water

Mix all ingredients. Bring to a boil and simmer for 5 minutes or until sauce thickens. Serve with fried dumplings, egg rolls or fried shrimps.

Yield: 2–3 cups.

Spanish Tomato Sauce

    ¼ cup olive oil
    1 tablespoon minced garlic
    ½ cup minced onion
    2 cups chopped fresh tomatoes,
       with seeds and skin remaining
    1 cup fish or chicken broth
salt and freshly ground pepper to
       taste

Heat oil and sauté garlic until brown, then onion until transparent and tomatoes until soft. Simmer for 10 minutes. Add broth, salt and pepper. Simmer for 1 hour in a covered pot. Serve with fish or chicken dishes.

Yield: 3 cups.

Misu Tomato Sauce

1 teaspoon cooking oil
1 teaspoon finely minced garlic
½ cup chopped onion
½ cup finely minced ripe
   tomatoes
2 tablespoons misu (salted bean
   paste, available in Oriental
   stores)
½ teaspoon apple cider vinegar
½ teaspoon freshly ground
   pepper

In a small skillet, heat oil and sauté garlic until light brown, then onion until transparent and tomatoes until soft. Add bean paste. Mix and mash the whole mixture with a fork. Add vinegar and pepper. Bring to a boil. Serve with boiled fish.

Yield: 1 cup.

Sausawang Suka • Vinaigrette Dip

¼ cup soy sauce
⅓ cup vinegar
3 cloves garlic, crushed
salt and pepper to taste
dash of red hot pepper (optional)

Mix all ingredients together. Serve with fried or roast meat and fish dishes.

Yield: About ⅔ cup.

Anatto Water or Anatto Oil

Anatto water or anatto oil is used to give food a reddish color. The water or oil may be used interchangeably in most recipes. The recipes given below may be increased proportionally should greater quantities be desired. A bottled preparation, known as achuete or achoite, is also available in many supermarkets and Hispanic food stores.

Anatto Water

1 tablespoon anatto seeds
4 tablespoons water

Place the seeds in the water and crush them between the fingers to release the red color. Let stand about 30 minutes. Strain the water and discard the seeds.

Anatto Oil

1 tablespoon anatto seeds
2 tablespoons oil

Fry the seeds in oil for several minutes. When the oil is cool enough to touch, crush the seeds. Let the mixture stand about 15 minutes; then strain and discard the seeds.

12
Desserts, Refreshments and Beverages

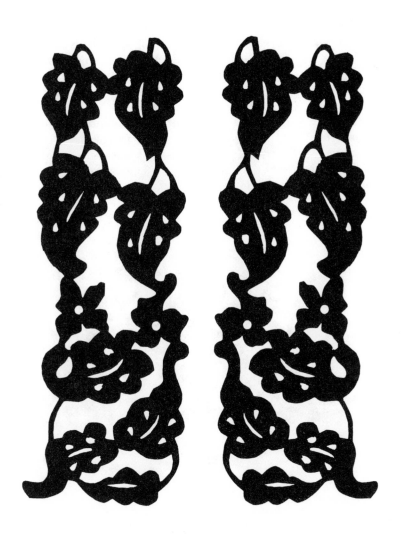

The Filipino fondness for sweets is evident in the numerous pastry shops and refreshment stands that can be found all over Manila. The brutal heat of the tropics almost demands that breaks be taken to cool the mind and refresh the body with iced treats and replenish energy with something sweet.

Kakanin is a generic term for the rice cakes that are available in many variations. Most have coconut milk as an ingredient, and most are "sticky sweet." They are frequently eaten as mid-morning or mid-afternoon snacks.

Pastilla de Leche is one of the most popular confections from the Philippines. The literal translation from the Spanish is "milk cake," but in fact the sweet is a mixture of sugar and milk. Other ingredients can be added, such as cashews in pastilla de casoy; peanuts in pastilla de mani; and lemon in pastilla de limón.

Yema (Spanish for "egg yolk") is another popular sweet. Legend has it that in Spanish times, egg white was used as a binding agent in the walls of churches and houses. What to do with the egg yolks? Cook them in sugar and roll them into balls that are firm on the outside and soft and moist on the inside.

Iced concoctions, the most notable of which is Halo-Halo, are almost a national institution. Everywhere in Manila, vendors with huge blocks of ice, machines for shaving and a wide assortment of sweets and flavorings offer respite from the blistering heat. The sight of one of these masterpieces being produced, the sound of ice being scraped, the coolness as the first spoonful touches the tongue and the mixture of flavors as the taste is experienced are all part of the ritual that cools the body and the mind.

Churros • Crullers

- 1 cup water
- 1½ teaspoons olive oil
- ½ teaspoon salt
- 1 cup all-purpose flour
- 2 cups vegetable or corn oil
- 1 cup confectioner's sugar (for sprinkling)

Bring to a boil a mixture of water, olive oil and salt. Pour in flour and mix very well. Place mixture inside a pastry bag. Press 1½ inches of the mixture at a time into a frying pan filled with hot vegetable or corn oil. Cook until brown. Sprinkle with sugar and serve.

Yield: About 30 crullers.

Ginataang Mongo • Bean Pudding

2 cups mung beans
2 cups glutinous sweet rice
1 cup coconut milk
1 cup coconut cream
5 tablespoons sugar

Brown the mung beans in a skillet until crisp. Crush the beans with a rolling pin. Mix the beans and the rice. In a medium pot, simmer the mixture in coconut milk over moderate heat for 30 minutes. Remove from heat. Add coconut cream and sugar.

Serves 8.

Suspiros de Casuy • Candied Cashew Nuts

2 cups sugar
1 cup water
2 tablespoons corn syrup
1 cup cashew nuts (or almonds
   or other nuts)

In a saucepan, caramelize sugar by boiling sugar and water together. Add corn syrup when mixture becomes sticky. Arrange nuts in a pastry pan and pour syrup on top. Gradually pull individual nuts so as to form threads. Pack in airtight bottles, jars or cans lined with wax paper.

Yield: 1 cup.

Fruit Salad, Philippine Style*

1½ cups heavy cream
1   8-ounce package cream cheese
3   14-ounce cans fruit cocktail,
    drained
1   14-ounce can pineapple
    chunks, drained
1   14-ounce can lychees, drained
1   cup preserved macapuno balls
    (sold in Philippine or Oriental
    stores)
1   8-ounce package unsalted
    chopped almonds
1½ cups fresh cubed apples
    (optional)

Mix heavy cream and cheese together to a smooth, saucelike consistency. Combine with all the other ingredients and blend well. Chill overnight and serve.

Serves 8.

---

*The Filipino taste is for canned fruit, a holdover from Colonial times. However, fresh fruits in season may be substituted if desired, sweetened to taste with honey or sugar.

Brazo de Mercedes • Creme-filled Log Cake

Filling

    5   cups milk
    1   cup sugar
    2   tablespoons unsalted butter
    1   tablespoon vanilla extract
    8   egg yolks
    ¼   cup toasted and finely ground
        cashew nuts

In a saucepan, simmer milk over low heat until reduced to 2 cups. Add sugar, butter and vanilla extract, stirring all the while. Remove from heat. Beat egg yolks in mixing bowl. To egg yolks, gradually add milk mixture by spoonfuls, beating all the while. Stir well to avoid curdling. Add cashew nuts and continue cooking entire mixture over low heat, stirring constantly, until mixture has consistency of a paste. Set aside.

Meringue

   10   egg whites
    1   cup sugar
    1   teaspoon vanilla extract

Preheat oven to 400° F. Beat egg whites until stiff. Gradually add 1 cup sugar, beating continuously. Stir in vanilla. Line large cookie sheet with parchment paper greased with butter and spread meringue on top. Bake until brown. Spread filling evenly on top of meringue and roll into a log. Brush with butter and brown again in oven.

Serves 6–8.

Palitao • Boiled Rice Cakes

2 cups sweet rice powder (sold
  in Oriental food stores)
½ cup water
1 cup grated coconut
¼ cup sesame seeds
1 cup sugar

Combine the sweet rice powder and ½ cup water and blend well. Boil 1½ quarts water in saucepan. Form the mixture into small balls, flatten, and drop into boiling water. When dough floats, remove from water and roll balls in grated coconut. Spread sesame seeds on cookie sheet and toast at 350° F until brown. Mix seeds with sugar and sprinkle on top of palitao.

Serves 8.

Maja Blanca • Coconut Cake

½ cup cornstarch
½ cup sugar
¼ cup water
2 cups coconut milk (sold in
  Oriental food stores)
3 cups grated coconut

Mix cornstarch and sugar in a bowl. Add water and stir. In a saucepan, bring coconut milk to a boil and gradually stir in cornstarch mixture. Boil for 5 minutes, until the starch is cooked. Pour into a buttered cake pan and let cool. Spread coconut on a baking sheet and toast at 350° F. until brown. Sprinkle cake with toasted grated coconut and serve.

Serves 4–6.

Polvoron • Powdered Milk Candy

3 cups sifted flour
1 cup sifted powdered milk
¾ cup sifted sugar
½ pound melted butter
1 teaspoon lemon or vanilla
extract

1 cup toasted flour.
1 cup powdered milk
3/4 c. sugar
1/2 lb. melted butter 3 small sticks
1 tsp vanilla extract
1/4 c pinipig
1/4 c pinipig
1/2 size

Toast flour in a heavy skillet or saucepan over moderate heat until light brown, stirring constantly. Remove from heat and cool. Add powdered milk, sugar, melted butter, lemon or vanilla extract. Form little cakes the diameter of a silver dollar but about a quarter-inch high. Wrap individually in wax paper.

Yield: About 20 candies.

Espasol • Sweet Rice Flour Cakes

4 cups sweet rice flour
1½ cups sugar
2 cans coconut milk
½ teaspoon salt

Toast the sweet rice flour on a cookie sheet. Bring sugar, coconut milk and salt to a boil. Add 3 cups toasted sweet rice flour. Mix well and cook until thick, stirring constantly. Remove from heat and transfer to board well sprinkled with some of the reserved sweet rice flour. With a rolling pin, flatten to about ¼ inch and cut into diamonds. Roll in the remaining rice flour.

Yield: 15 to 20 cakes.

Pianono • Coco-Choco Roll

¼   cup butter
⅓   cup ground unsalted almonds
1   cup coconut flakes
12-ounce can condensed milk
1   cup sifted flour
⅓   cup cocoa
¼   teaspoon salt
1   teaspoon baking soda
1   cup sugar
3   eggs, separated
⅓   cup cold water
1   teaspoon vanilla
confectioner's sugar

Line a 10- by 15-inch jelly-roll pan with foil. Preheat oven to 375° F. Melt butter and pour into foiled pan. Mix nuts and coconut flakes and sprinkle evenly in pan. Drizzle with condensed milk. Sift together flour, cocoa, salt, baking soda and sugar. Beat egg yolks in bowl until fluffy. Blend sifted dry ingredients, water and vanilla and beat for another minute. Beat egg whites separately until stiff and fold into mixture. Pour into pan and bake for 20 minutes or until cake is done. Sprinkle with confectioner's sugar. Transfer to a cookie sheet, roll in jelly-roll fashion and wrap with a towel to set until cool. Transfer to a serving platter and sprinkle with more confectioner's sugar. Slice to serve.

Serves 6–8.

Maruya • Banana Fritters

 1 cup sifted flour
 1 teaspoon baking powder
½ teaspoon salt
 2 tablespoons sugar
 4 tablespoons milk
⅓ cup water
 1 egg, beaten
 4 ripe bananas
½ cup cooking oil
powdered sugar (optional)

Sift flour, baking powder, salt and sugar. Add milk, water and egg to the dry ingredients and mix until batter is smooth.

Peel the bananas and slice lengthwise into 4 pieces. Dip in the batter and roll lightly in flour. Deep fry in cooking oil, browning evenly. Drain and serve with powdered sugar if desired.

Yield: 16 fritters.

Tocino del Cielo • Confection of Eggs and Syrup

  4 cups sugar
  3 cups water
25 egg yolks
  8 ounces butter

Preheat oven to 325° F. In a saucepan, boil sugar and water together until they form a syrup. Line a baking pan, mold or small individual molds with ½ cup of the syrup.* Mix remaining syrup (now at room temperature) with the 25 egg yolks. Blend well. Add butter. Strain and pour mixture into the pan or mold previously lined with syrup.

    Fill a larger pan with water and put the pan or molds containing mixture inside the larger pan. Place in oven and bake until thick and set. Let cool before unmolding.

Serves 8–10.

Yema • Egg Balls

  4 cups milk
 ¾ cup sugar
10 egg yolks
  1 teaspoon vanilla extract
  2 cups confectioner's sugar

In a saucepan, simmer milk over low heat until it is reduced to 1 cup. Stir in sugar until well blended. Turn off heat and let cool. Mix 3 tablespoons of the simmered milk with the egg yolks and then add this mixture gradually to the milk in the pan. Stir in vanilla extract and continue stirring over low heat until mixture thickens. Remove from heat and let cool. Shape into balls, using one tablespoon of the mixture to make one ball. Roll finished balls in confectioner's sugar.

Serves 6–8.

---

*Small individual molds are usually used, then the mixture is unmolded into small soufflé cups before serving.

Gulo-Gulong Kamote • Deep Fried Sweet Potato

- 1 cup flour
- 2 teaspoons baking powder
- 1 tablespoon sugar
- ¼ teaspoon salt
- 2 cups sweet potatoes sliced thin
  in ¼-inch squares
- 1 egg
- ¼ cup milk
- 1 cup cooking oil
- 1 cup sugar

Mix and sift flour, baking powder, sugar and salt. Add remaining ingredients. Form 3-inch patties and deep fry. Drain and sprinkle with sugar to coat before serving.

Yield: About 48 pieces.

Matamis Na Saging • Banana Sweets

    1   cup brown sugar
    2   cups water
    ¼   teaspoon salt
    4   ripe plantains cut lengthwise
        into ⅛-inch-thick slices (sliced
        sweet potatoes may be
        substituted)
    8   ounces sweet butter
sherry

In a saucepan, combine sugar, water and salt and cook over medium heat until a
thick syrup forms. Simmer. Add plantain slices and butter to the syrup and
continue simmering for 15 minutes. Lace each individual serving with a tablespoon of sherry and serve at once.

Yield: 25 pieces.

Bunuelos • Sweet Fritters

    1   cup water
    8   ounces sweet butter
    ½   teaspoon salt
    1   cup sifted flour
    5   eggs
    2   cups vegetable or corn oil
sugar for coating

In a deep saucepan, boil water, butter and salt. Stir in flour and mix in one
direction until mixture pulls away from the sides of the pan and forms a solid
mass. Turn off heat and stir in eggs one after the other.
    Heat oil in a deep frying pan. Drop the mixture ½ teaspoon at a time into the
pan and fry until brown. Drain on paper towel and roll in sugar.

Serves 10.

Lenguas de Gato • Cats' Tongue Pastries

½ cup sweet butter
½ cup sugar
2 egg whites
1⅓ cups all-purpose flour
¼ teaspoon salt
½ teaspoon vanilla extract

Preheat oven to 400° F. Cream butter and blend with sugar. Beat the egg whites until foamy. Add egg whites gradually to butter and sugar mixture. Add flour and salt. Add vanilla extract and mix well. Using a cake-decorating tube, form dough into oblong, tonguelike shapes. Drop each piece onto a cookie sheet lined with greased parchment paper. Bake for 10 minutes. Remove and let cool.

Yield: About 50 pieces.

Sans Rival • Napoleon Layered Cake

5   egg whites
1   cup sugar
1½ cup chopped unsalted cashews
    or almonds
½   teaspoon vanilla

Preheat oven to 350° F. Grease and flour heavily three 18-by-15-inch cookie sheets. Set aside.

   Beat egg whites until stiff. Add sugar gradually and continue beating. Fold in chopped nuts and vanilla. Spread thin in prepared pans and bake for 20 minutes or until golden brown. Loosen and slide wafers to a flat surface and cool. Prepare filling.

Filling

¼   cup water
⅔   cup sugar
5   eggs, separated
1   cup (8 ounces) butter
2   tablespoons rum
½   cup chopped cashew nuts

Boil water and sugar until it forms a syrup that spins a thread. Beat egg whites until thick. Pour syrup into egg yolks in thin streams while beating. Remove and chill in refrigerator for 20 to 30 minutes. Cream butter and blend into egg yolk mixture. Add rum. Fill and cover wafers with filling. Sprinkle top with chopped cashews. Serve chilled.

Serves 8–10.

Leche Flan • Crème Caramel

Caramel

  1   cup sugar
  ¼ cup water

Caramelize sugar in a saucepan by boiling with water and stirring continously over medium heat until sugar is melted. Pour caramelized syrup into flan mold or custard cups,* tilting the mold to make sure the whole surface is covered.

Custard

 12 egg yolks
  2 13-ounce cans evaporated milk
  1 14-ounce can sweetened
     condensed milk
  1 teaspoon vanilla

In a large bowl, combine all custard ingredients. Stir lightly when mixing to prevent bubbles or foam from forming. Strain slowly while pouring into caramel-lined flan mold. Preheat oven to 325° F. Cover mold with tin foil. Put mold in a bigger tray filled with water. Bake in oven for 1 hour or until mixture is firm. Cool before unmolding on a platter.

Note: for Macapuno Flan, follow same procedure as Leche Flan. When serving, top with macapuno (coconut sold in the United States as preserves).

Serves 10.

---

*Any ovenware dish about 2 inches deep may be used.

Maja Blanca Maiz • Coconut Corn Cake

  2 cups corn kernels, fresh or
    canned
 10 cups milk
  1 cup white sugar
  ½ cup fresh coconut oil
  1 teaspoon toasted anise
  3 cups grated coconut meat (for
    latik)
  1 cup latik*

Put corn kernels in a food processor. Blend, then strain in a sieve. To the strained corn, add milk and sugar and cook over medium heat. Stir constantly and add fresh coconut oil little by little to avoid burning. When thick, add toasted anise and mix well. Pour into serving platter greased with coconut oil. When cool, serve with latik.

Serves 6–8.

*To make latik: Boil pure coconut milk until oil is formed, together with a cheeselike precipitate that becomes brown in color. This precipitate is the latik. Drain the oil from the latik. Fresh coconut oil is used as an ingredient in some dishes and for greasing plates and molds, while latik is used as a topping for certain native delicacies.

Petits Fours

¾ cup chopped unsalted cashew
    nuts
2 tablespoons all-purpose flour
½ cup sugar
2 egg yolks, slightly beaten
2 tablespoons heavy cream
⅓ cup butter, melted
1 egg white, stiffly beaten
powdered sugar and glacé cherries
    for decoration

Preheat oven to 350° F. Mix the dry ingredients thoroughly in a bowl. Make a well in the center and add egg yolks, cream and melted butter. Mix until well blended, then add egg white. Pour into 1¼-inch-diameter fluted paper cups and bake for 12 to 15 minutes. Sprinkle a small amount of powdered sugar on each petit four and decorate each with a cherry to serve.

Yield: 40 pieces

Bibingka • Flat Cake

¾ cup granulated sugar
1¼ cups coconut milk (sold in
Oriental stores)
3 eggs, beaten
2 cups all-purpose flour
1 teaspoon salt
4 tablespoons baking powder
½ cup grated Edam cheese
½ cup melted butter or margarine
to baste
sugar to sprinkle, enough to cover
cake
½ cup grated coconut

Preheat oven to 375°F. Mix the sugar with the coconut milk in a bowl. Make sure sugar has dissolved. Add beaten eggs.

In a bowl, sift the flour. Add salt and baking powder and sift again. Combine the egg mixture with the flour mixture. Beat well. Pour into a baking pan. Bake for 15 minutes. Sprinkle with cheese and bake 20 minutes more, brushing twice with margarine while baking. When done, brush again with margarine and sprinkle with sugar. Serve with grated coconut.

Serves 4.

Bibingkang Kanin • Rice Cake

- 3 cups coconut milk (sold in Oriental stores)
- 2 cups sweet rice (sold in Oriental stores)
- 1 teaspoon salt
- 1 cup brown sugar
- butter to grease pan
- ¾ cup coconut cream (sold in Oriental stores)
- 2 tablespoons anise seeds

Preheat oven to 350° F. Bring coconut milk to a boil in a saucepan. Add sweet rice and salt. Cook over moderate heat until dry, stirring constantly to keep from burning. When dry, lower heat and add ¼ cup brown sugar.

Grease cake pan with butter and pour in mixture. Top with coconut cream and ¾ cup brown sugar. Sprinkle with anise seeds. Bake for 20 minutes.

Serves 6–8.

Cassava Pudding

    2 pounds grated cassava
  one 14-ounce can condensed milk
  one 13-ounce can evaporated milk
  one 16-ounce can less 6
       tablespoons coconut cream
       (sold in Oriental stores)
    2 cups coconut milk (sold in
       Oriental stores)
grated coconut
   ½ cup sugar
    5 eggs

Topping

    2 egg yolks, beaten
    6 tablespoons coconut cream
    6 tablespoons condensed milk

Preheat oven to 350° F. In a mixing bowl, combine pudding ingredients (save 6 tablespoons coconut cream for topping). Mix well. Pour mixture into a buttered 11¾-inch shallow rectangular cake pan and bake for approximately 30 minutes.

   Mix the topping ingredients well and spread evenly on top of pudding and continue baking for another 25 minutes.

Serves 10.

Puto Maya • Coconut Rice Cake

A rice dessert or afternoon snack named after the native bird, the maya.

- 3 cups sweet rice (sold in Oriental stores)
- 6 cups coconut milk (sold in Oriental stores)
- 1 cup brown sugar
- 2 cups grated coconut

In a 6-quart saucepan, bring sweet rice and coconut milk to a boil, then lower heat and simmer until liquid is absorbed and rice is soft. Place on a large platter. Mix brown sugar and grated coconut. Serve as a topping or side dish with the rice cake.

Serves 6–8.

Putong Puti • Rice Muffins

- 2 cups rice flour
- 3 teaspoons baking powder
- 1 cup white sugar
- ½ teaspoon salt
- 2 cups coconut milk (sold in Oriental stores)
- 1 teaspoon anise seeds
- 1 cup grated coconut

Sift first four ingredients together. In a mixing bowl, add coconut milk to sifted ingredients and blend well to make a smooth mixture. Add anise seeds. Mix and blend thoroughly and fill greased muffin pans ⅔ full. Cook in a steamer for 30 minutes. Test for doneness. Muffins are done when toothpick or cake tester inserted in center comes out clean. Serve topped with grated coconut.

Serves 4.

Pastillas de Leche • Milk Candy

    4   quarts milk
1½   cups sugar
    1   tablespoon lemon rind
sugar to coat

In a deep saucepan, simmer milk and continue stirring until it is reduced to one quart. Add sugar and lemon rind and continue to simmer over low heat until the mixture forms a solid mass. Place the mixture on a sugared board and spread out into a rectangle ½ inch high. Divide rectangle into pieces measuring ½ inch wide by 2 inches long. Roll pieces in sugar and wrap individually in tissue paper.

Yield: 25 pieces

Pastillas de Casoy • Cashew Nut Milk Candy

one 8-ounce can condensed milk
    1   cup chopped cashew nuts or
        almonds
    1   tablespoon sugar
    1   tablespoon lemon extract

Combine condensed milk, nuts and sugar and simmer until thick. Add lemon extract and continue stirring until mixture forms a solid mass. Spread with rolling pin on a sugared board and roll into a rectangular shape ½ inch high. Cut into desired pieces and wrap in tissue paper.

Yield: 2 cups.

Ginataang Bilo-Bilo • Rice Balls with Coconut Milk

 1 cup glutinous rice flour
    (malagkit, sold in Oriental
    stores)
⅓ cup water
 3 cups coconut milk (sold in
    Oriental stores), thinned with
    ½ cup water
 1 cup sugar
 2 cups large-pearl tapioca
1½ cups coconut cream (sold in
    Oriental stores)

Blend flour and water into a dough. Shape into balls ¼ inch in diameter.

In a large pot, boil coconut milk, sugar and tapioca. When tapioca is transparent, add the rice balls. When the rice balls are soft but firm, add coconut cream and boil for 5 more minutes. Serve hot.

Serves 6–8.

Ginataang Mais • Corn with Coconut Milk

 3 ears young corn or 1½ cups
    creamed corn
 1 cup coconut milk
 6 cups water
¾ cup sugar
¾ cup sweet rice (sold in Oriental
    stores)

Remove corn kernels from cob if using fresh corn. In a pan, combine coconut milk, water, sugar and sweet rice. Simmer for 20 to 30 minutes or until all liquid is absorbed and rice is soft. Add corn and cook for another 10 to 15 minutes or until corn is mushy. Serve hot or cold.

Serves 6–8.

Pastillas de Mani • Peanut Milk Candy

1   cup freshly ground unsalted
     peanuts
1   cup milk
¾   cup sugar

Combine all ingredients and simmer over low heat, stirring constantly, until a solid mass is formed. Transfer to a sugared board and spread the mixture with a rolling pin into a rectangular shape ½ inch high. Cut into ½-inch-wide by 2-inch-long pieces. Wrap individually in tissue paper if desired.

Yield: 20 pieces.

Gulaman at Sago • Tapioca with Coconut Milk

1   packet unflavored gelatin
1   cup sugar
2   teaspoons lemon extract
1   cup tapioca
6   cups water
1½   cups coconut milk diluted with
      4 cups water

Prepare gelatin according to directions. Add sugar and lemon extract. Mix well. Let set in a shallow container.

Boil tapioca in 6 cups water until tapioca becomes clear. Cool and drain. Mix tapioca, gelatin (cut into ½-inch squares) and coconut milk and serve.

Serves 8.

Halo-Halo Supreme

For Filipinos, Halo-Halo is the ultimate warm weather refreshment. In a tall glass, a great variety of cooked fruits and sweet vegetables are layered and topped with shaved ice. The finished product appeals to the eye as well as the palate.

   A variety of fruits (fresh, frozen, preserved or canned) can be used. Most can be bought in Oriental stores.

   1   tablespoon kaong or . . .
   1   tablespoon nangka (jackfruit) or . . .
   1   tablespoon macapuno or . . .
   1   tablespoon sweetened kidney beans
   1   tablespoon sweetened garbanzos (chick peas)
   1   tablespoon sweetened plantains
   1   tablespoon ube or yam
   1   tablespoon custard or crème caramel
   1   tablespoon sweetened corn kernels
crushed ice to fill glass
   ⅓   cup evaporated milk
   1   small scoop ice cream (vanilla or mocha)
1 or 2 maraschino cherries

Fill the bottom half of a tall glass with a tablespoon of each sweetened fruit or vegetable. Add crushed ice to cover the top half of the glass. Pour ⅓ cup of milk on the ice.* Top with a small scoop of ice cream. Put a cherry on top. Serve with long-stemmed spoons.

Serves 1–2.

---

*Ten ice cubes, crushed, mixed with 1 cup milk in an electric blender will make "snow," which can be used in place of the crushed ice and ⅓ cup evaporated milk.

Ginataang Halo-Halo
• Halo-Halo* with Coconut milk

     4 cups water
   1½ cups coconut milk (sold in
        Oriental stores)
     ½ cup sugar
     1 cup diced sweet potatoes
     1 cup diced plantains
     3 tablespoons water
     1 cup sweet rice powder (sold in
        Oriental stores)
     ¼ cup tapioca (quick-cooking
        type)
     1 cup jackfruit (sold preserved in
        Oriental stores), cut into strips

In a medium pot, bring the water and coconut milk to a boil. Add ¼ cup sugar and simmer. Add sweet potatoes and plantains and simmer until half done. Add 3 tablespoons water to sweet rice powder. Take a little of the mixture at a time and form into balls the size of hazelnuts. Drop balls into the simmering mixture. Add cooked tapioca, ¼ cup sugar and jackfruit. Stir and cook for 5 minutes. Serve hot or cold.

Serves 1–2.

---

*Halo-halo literally means a mixture; in this case a mixture of fruit.

Pineapple-Calamansi Punch
• Pineapple-Lemon Punch

2½ cups pineapple juice
 ½ cup lemon juice
 1 cup ice
 6 tablespoons sugar
 ⅛ to ½ cup light rum
orange slices and maraschino
     cherries to garnish

Mix all ingredients except orange slices and cherries. Serve cold, garnished with orange slices and maraschino cherries.

Serves 5–6.

Guayabano Chiller

one 16-ounce can guayabano juice
     (sold in Oriental food stores)
sugar to taste
 ¼ cup lemon juice
 2 quarts water
rum (optional)

Mix all ingredients. Sweeten to taste and serve with ice cubes.

Yield: 10 cups.

Iced Melon

    1 cantaloupe or honeydew
       melon
    1 cup water
    ¼ cup honey
    ½ cup milk

Grate melon.˙ Add water and honey. Add milk and mix well. Chill and serve.

                                                    Serves 2.

Salabat • Ginger Tea

    ½ pound fresh ginger, sliced
    5 cups water
    1 cup brown sugar

Boil all ingredients together. Add more water if tea is too strong. Strain and serve hot.

                                                    Serves 4–5.

˙A melon scraper may be obtained at Oriental food stores, or use any type of fruit shaver.

Tsokolate • Chocolate Drink

one 18.6-ounce pack chocolate
containing 6 tablets
(recommended brand is Ibarra,
which can be purchased at
Hispanic food stores)
  6 cups milk
  6 egg yolks

Cut chocolate tablets into small pieces. Boil the milk and add all the chocolate. Stir constantly till chocolate is liquefied. Beat the egg yolks. Add them to the pot. Then beat the whole mixture until frothy. Serve hot.

Serves 4–6.

Glossary

Achara—pickled fruits or vegetables served as a relish with grated green papaya or sauerkraut.

Achuete or Achiote—anatto seeds used to give food a reddish color. Seeds are soaked in water to extract the color. Usually available in bottles in most supermarkets or Hispanic food stores.

Adobo—a generic term for cooking meat, fish or vegetables in garlic, vinegar, soy sauce and pepper. It is the name of the dish as well as the style of cooking.

Alimango—a variety of crab with large pincers.

Alimasag—smaller crab than the *alimango*.

Apritada—meat dish with tomato sauce and vegetables; a Spanish-influenced dish.

Arroz—Spanish word for "rice."

Asado—a meat dish cooked with tomatoes, onions and other seasonings.

Baboy—Tagalog term for "pork" or "pig."

Bagoong—salty, fermented sauce or paste made from small shrimps or fish, used as an accompaniment to main dishes; also known as anchovy sauce. It is available regular or sautéed.

Bistek—beefsteak.

Buko—a young coconut.

Calamansi—a small limelike fruit found in the tropics. Lemon is the best substitute.

Cassava—an edible, starchy root used in making bread or tapioca.

Chicharon—crisp fried pork rind or skin.

Dilis—long-jawed anchovy.

Caldereta—goat-meat stew.

Camaron rebosado—shelled shrimps (with tail on) dipped in a batter and deep fried.

Chorizo de Bilbao—Spanish sausage used for flavoring dishes.

Embutido—ground meat roll, usually made with ground pork stuffed with ham, pickles, eggs and raisins.

Empanada—meat turnover with ground beef, chopped olives, raisins and a slice of hard-boiled egg.

Empanadita—small turnover with honey and nuts.

Ensalada—Spanish term for "salad."

Escabeche—fish in sweet-and-sour sauce.

Estofado—stewed meat dish cooked with vinegar, sugar and other spices.

Frito—Tagalog term for "fried."

Flan—custard made of milk and egg yolks.

Fritada—see *Apritada*.

Gallina—Spanish word for "chicken."

Gata—Tagalog word for "coconut milk."

Ginataan—method of cooking food in coconut milk.

Guisado—Tagalog word for "sautéed."

Hamon—Tagalog spelling of the Spanish word for ham (*jamón*).

Inihaw—Tagalog term for "charcoal-broiled."

Kangkong—green, smooth-leafed vegetable native to the Philippines. It has a flavor that is milder than spinach and a texture similar to watercress.

Kare-Kare—Philippine meat-vegetable stew with ox tail, beef or tripe, eggplant, banana buds and other vegetables cooked in peanut sauce and ground toasted rice.

Kawali—native skillet or pan.

Kuhol—Tagalog word for "snails."

Kutsay—Tagalog word for "leeks."

Labong—Tagalog word for "bamboo shoots."

Leche flan—*leche* is the Spanish word for milk; a milk and egg yolk custard.

Lechón—roast suckling pig.

Lengua—Spanish word for "tongue."

Lomo—beef loin.

Longaniza—native sausage.

Lumpia—Philippine egg rolls.

Manok—Tagalog word for "chicken."

Mechado—meat into which long strips of fat have been inserted, then simmered in tomato sauce and spices.

Menudo—diced pork and liver stew with vegetables.

Merienda—afternoon tea.

Miki—rice noodle.

Misua or Miswa—threadlike wheat noodle; a vermicelli.

Misu—soybean paste.

Mongo—mung beans.

Morcon—beef meat roll stuffed with eggs, ham, pickles and sausages.

Nilaga—Tagalog for "boiled."

Paksiw—fish or meat cooked in vinegar, garlic and hot cooking peppers.

Pansit—noodle dish.

Pastillas—sweets in the form of little bars made of milk and sugar, with or without nuts.

Patis—very salty, amber-colored, thin liquid extract from salted and fermented seafood (usually fish). Very similar to the Vietnamese *nuoc mam* and the Thai *nampla*, which may be substituted.

Pesa—fish or meat dish with vegetables simmered with fresh ginger.

Pipino—Tagalog for "cucumber."

Pochero—dish of boiled beef, chicken, dumplings and vegetables, which is similar to the Spanish *cocida.*

Pusit—Tagalog word for "squid."

Puto—steamed rice cake.

Relleno—Spanish word for "stuffed;" used for any stuffed dish.

Salabat—ginger tea.

Sili—long green cooking pepper.

Sinigang—sour soup dish of meat or fish with vegetables, seasoned with tomatoes, onions and lemon juice.

Siomai—dumplings.

Sitao—string beans, a yard-long bean.

Sotanghon—transparent bean noodles; also known as cellophane noodles.

Sugpo—giant tiger prawn.

Talaba—Tagalog term for "oyster."

Talong—Tagalog term for "eggplant."

Tapa—dried meat cured with salt and vinegar.

Tausi—black soy beans, salted and fermented.

Tinola—fish or meat dish flavored with ginger.

Togue—bean sprout.

Tokwa—soy bean cake.

Tulya—freshwater clams.

Ubod—hearts of palm.

Upo—Philippine gourd.

Yema—Spanish for "egg yolk."

Appendix

Sources for Filipino Ingredients

Here is a sample listing of some sources of Filipino cooking ingredients in selected North American cities. For more complete and current listings, consult your local Yellow Pages under "Groceries—Oriental," "Groceries—Hispanic," or "Groceries—Filipino."

California

M & M Oriental Foods
    (Phil-Oriental Foods)
635-B E. Arrow Highway
Azusa 91702
(213) 339-8234; 334-9652

Manila Oriental Goods & Bake
    Shop
22102 S. Main St.
Carson 90745
(213) 518-1238; 518-1239

Tambuli Oriental Foods
108 W. Carson Street
Carson 90745
(213) 549-4251

Philippine Plaza
17610 S. Pioneer Boulevard
Cerritos 90701
(213) 924-1690

Filipino Market
2525 Santa Fe Avenue
Long Beach 90801
(213) 426-3509

Filipino Oriental Mart
1804 Temple Street
Los Angeles 90052
(213) 413-0217

Lorenzana Food Corp.
4921-25 Santa Monica Boulevard
Los Angeles 90028
(213) 660-4493

Philippine Grocery
4929 Mission Street
San Francisco 94101
(415) 584-4465

Phil-Mart
109 King Plaza Shopping Center
San Francisco 94101
(415) 878-1611

Simex International
331 Clement Street
San Francisco 94101
(415) 668-1233

Illinois

Philippine Food Corp.
4547 N. Ravenswood
Chicago 60625
(312) 784-7447

Philippine World
1051-57 W. Belmont Avenue
Chicago 60657
(312) 248-5100

Oriental Food Mart
Westlake Plaza
2208 Bloomingdale Road
Glendale Heights 60137
(312) 980-1779

Massachusetts

Oriental Giftland
72 Harrison Avenue
Boston 02109
(617) 426-0773

Michigan

Phil-Asian Tropical Food Mart
4638 Woodward
Detroit 48233
(313) 831-7530

Oriental Food Groceries
18919 West Seventh Mile
Detroit 48233
(313) 534-7773

Minnesota

Phil-Oriental Imports, Inc.
476 Lexington Parkway
St. Paul 55104
(612) 646-5479

New Jersey

Mira-San Oriental Food Store
530 Newark Avenue
Jersey City 07306
(201) 656-4330

Fil-Am Food Mart, Inc.
685 Newark Avenue
Jersey City 07306
(201) 963-0461

New York

Mabuhay
524 Ninth Avenue
New York 10018
(212) 868-6663

E.V. Varieties
349 Hempstead Avenue
Elmont 11003
(516) 488-6178

Phil-Am Food Mart
40-03 70th Street
Woodside 11377
(212) 899-1797; 899-1808

Oriental Foods
526 Ninth Avenue
New York 10018
(store has no phone)

Sampaguita Food Store
347 E. 14th Street
New York 10011
(212) 673-3788

House of Oriental Food
52 Route 303 North
Blauvelt 10913
(914) 359-3306

Cindee's Filipino Grocery
185-02 Hillside Avenue
Jamaica 11423
(212) 454-3834

AsianAttic, Inc.
8 Briarwood Terrace
Albany 12203
(518) 456-4803

Ohio

Bayanihan Food, Inc.
625 Bolivar
Cleveland 44101
(216) 781-2468

Pennsylvania

Phil-Am Food Mart
5601 Camac
Philadelphia 19104
(215) 927-7373

Chinese & Oriental Food Product
        Research Inc.
117 N. 10th Street
Philadelphia 19107
(215) 922-6062; 922-6657

Texas

Little Home Bakery & Grocery
2109 Parker Road, Suite 202A
Plano
Dallas 75023
(214) 596-3382

Washington

The Philippine Best
10303 Greenwood North
Seattle 98103
(206) 782-9011

Fiesta Filipina Store
522 6th South
Seattle 98101
(206) 624-6160

Washington, D.C., Area

Manila Mart
3610 Lee Highway
Arlington, Va. 22207
(301) 528-0300

Canada

Filipino Market
4 Irwin Avenue
Toronto, Ontario
(416 967-6532)

Philippine Products Sari-Sari Store
507-B Gladstone Avenue
Ottawa, Ontario
(telephone # not available)

Philippine Sari-Sari Store
4939 Côte des Neiges
Montreal, Quebec
(514) 733-0625

Index